PERSUADED

by the SEVEN DEADLY SINS of DECISION MAKING and INFLUENCE

Kenneth J. Taylor

39 Consulting, LLC

Atlanta, GA

Kenneth J. Taylor/39 Consulting, LLC
3395 Wolf Willow Close
Milton, GA 30004
www.39consulting.com

Ordering Information:

Quantity sales and special discounts are available on quantity
purchases by corporations, associations, and others. For
details, visit www.39consulting.com.

Persuaded/ Kenneth J. Taylor. —1st ed.

ISBN 978-0-9986788-0-1

To Kellie, Alex, Zoe,
Mom and Dad

Thank you for your love and unwavering support.

CONTENTS

Introduction.. 1

How to Read This Book 3

CHAPTER ONE

Theory Meets Practicality 7

CHAPTER TWO

The Science of Decision Making 11

CHAPTER THREE

The First Deadly Sin: Justifying...................................... 15

CHAPTER FOUR

The Second Deadly Sin: Stereotyping 49

CHAPTER FIVE

The Third Deadly Sin: False-Cause 77

CHAPTER SIX

The Fourth Deadly Sin: Familiararity 111

CHAPTER SEVEN

The Fifth Deadly Sin: Doubling Down 135

CHAPTER EIGHT

The Sixth Deadly Sin: Inflexibility 161

CHAPTER NINE

The Seventh Deadly Sin: Risk Aversion.......................... 185

Conclusion: 221

Notes & Refrences.. 225

Index... 259

"Almost all painful feelings have their source in an incorrect way of looking at reality. When you uproot erroneous views, suffering ceases."
—The Buddha

INTRODUCTION

Have you ever been persuaded to do something that wasn't in your best interest? Of course you have. We all have, because we are all susceptible to the errors I call the seven deadly sins of decision making and influence.

On the flip side, these "sins" are also ripe with opportunity to influence the choices of others. This is the power of persuasion. Savvy marketers, sales people, and political strategists use the techniques covered in this book often, and with great effectiveness.

This book is not about formal decision theory. Why? Because theory is useless in everyday life. For example, the definition of *normative decision theory* comes with this caveat: "assuming an ideal, fully informed, rational decision maker who is able to compute with perfect accuracy." How many ideal, fully informed, rational decision makers are there on the planet? Not many. And in my experience, there aren't very many people who compute with perfect accuracy, either. The caveat might as well read, "Assume a perfect world."

Information about how we make decisions is often presented in dry scholarly material written in a formal style and filled with psycho-technical terms. It is not light reading; I can assure you. The great misfortune here is that the information is so valuable. Frankly, the world would be a much better place if we all improve our decision making... even a little. My goal is to present this information in a manner that is easier to digest for people like you and me. People who want practical solutions and techniques to make better decisions and influence the decision making of others.

Through real-world and (I hope) enjoyable stories, you will learn that most of our decisions are based on snap judgments and unconscious biases that can lead us astray. My intention is to give you a better understanding of the seven deadly sins so you can make better choices and have the tools to avoid becoming the victim of a poor decision made by someone else.

HOW TO READ THIS BOOK

The Seven Deadly Sins

We will reveal the seven most frequent and threatening decision-making mistakes or "sins." There are more, but these are the big ones. Each chapter explores what to look for (the sin), why it happens (the science) and what to do about it (the practical real-world response). While I drew on the tactics of practical influence practitioners (e.g. crooks, pick-up artists, politicians and sales people), I tied their methods back to science through my personal research and in collaboration with psychology professors Dr. Jeannine Jannot and Dr. Frank Provenzano.

On the Flip Side

Information is of little use unless we apply it. Each chapter in this book includes a section called *On the Flip Side* with practical suggestions and persuasion techniques.

If you would like to try a technique, first test it in a low-risk situation with no long-lasting negative consequences. For example, I learned a particularly powerful body language technique and decided to try it on my friend and co-worker, Fran. I couldn't tell him what I was doing ahead of time, of course, so as soon as I detected a response, I quickly stopped and explained what I was up to. Fran is a good friend, and I knew he'd be interested in what I'd learned. I wouldn't have tried it with my boss during my annual performance review!

If the technique proves unsuccessful for you in a low-value situation, no harm/no foul. When a technique does work for you in a trial run, understand that it might not work all the time and in every situation. Like anything else in life, mastering these techniques takes practice and patience. I suggest you begin by practicing one or two techniques before moving on to others.

As you read through the *On the Flip Side* sections, think about situations when people have used these approaches on you. When I uncovered these techniques, I realized how many times I had fallen for them. It was a rude awakening. Professional influence practitioners are practiced and skilled in the art of influence and will clean your clock if you are not careful. One purpose of this book is to help you identify when a professional influencer is using persuasion techniques on you. The good news is, once you learn these methods, they become much easier to spot. Awareness is your greatest defense.

Momentary Lapses of Reason

Five notable occasions trigger autopilot cognitive processing. This is when we activate our unconscious mind to make decisions. Unfortunately, our unconscious mind is where our blind spots are hiding, leading us to make mistakes in judgment. I call these momentary lapses of reason. The occasions are as follows:

- When we have too little information
- When we have too much information
- When we are emotionally aroused
- When we are pressed for time
- When we are afraid.

Between each of the seven deadly sins are short passages on the momentary lapses of reason, including autopilot. They are in no particular order and each lapse of reason could be associated with each sin. I encourage you to think of a time when your decision making was influenced by one of these occasions.

Kenneth J. Taylor

THEORY MEETS PRACTICALITY

I wrote this book for three reasons.

Reason #1:

I'm a marketer. My job is to influence people to choose a specific product, service, idea, or candidate, and this choice usually occurs when I am not present. I have studied decision making in the real world for over two decades and have become both fascinated and frustrated with the irrationality of consumer and customer decision making... as well as with my own and that of my colleagues. About ten years ago, to get a better grasp on consumer behavior and to improve my marketing skill set, I immersed myself in the science and psychology of decision making.

I read every marketing and psychology book I could get my hands on. These books were wonderful in providing scientific theories, studies, definitions, and classifications, but they often lacked practical application. For that, I turned to books and articles about con artists, pick-up artists, crooks, politicians, and expert sales people. These practitioners of persuasion in the real world are more motivated to find techniques to make the con, get the girl, win the election, or make the sale. They have fine-tuned their techniques over hundreds of years to determine what actually works on us unsuspecting victim-types. My research uncovered how often I have been guilty of committing one of the seven deadly sins and how often I have been the victim of persuasion tactics. Let's just say a lot. I'll share some of those stories with you in the book. Admittedly, I'm a bit of a mad scientist. When I came across an interesting persuasion technique, I found a way to test it in the market. When there wasn't an opportunity to test an idea in the market, I'd try it on my peers (sorry guys!). Some techniques worked for me, some didn't. After years of learning, testing, reading, and reacting, I had a pretty good handle on persuasion and the science or psychology behind it. I decided to write this book to share what I have learned.

Reason #2:

The second reason I became interested in the topic of decision making, and decided to write this book, is that I saw successful people making bad decisions on a consistent basis.

Irrational decision making is not exclusive to consumer behavior. We all have a friend or relative (or friends and relatives) who consistently makes poor life choices. We almost expect these people to make mistakes because frankly their track record supports that expectation. My friend Jay calls them "knuckleheads." When I began working with senior-level business leaders, I noticed that the decision making of these smart, well-educated people was often just as irrational and erratic as my knuckleheaded friends. Unfortunately, the consequences are much greater when a CEO or a political leader makes a poor decision.

This got my attention. I had always assumed the people at the very top were consistently good decision makers. Making good decisions was what got them to the top of the pyramid, right? That was and is simply not true. Many leaders are brilliant people with blind spots that affect their judgment. Others are knuckleheads who rose to the top by benefiting from the poor judgment of someone else in power. Have you ever met a "successful" person and wondered how on earth he or she made it?

Reason #3:

Most of the books and articles I read while learning about decision making were academic and somewhat dry. Others were a bit lighter, but failed to provide practical tips on how to persuade decision makers. That's the whole point, isn't it? It doesn't matter if you are selling something or being sold something, understanding how we make decisions and how to influence decision making is a very practical and useful field of knowledge.

I decided to try to explain the science behind decision making in an engaging way, and then show you how to use it. *On the Flip Side* of each chapter offers tips on how to leverage each "sin" to persuade a decision maker. These techniques can be very powerful, so use them wisely, with positive intentions and discretion.

After reading this book, you will begin to notice how often we are influenced by the seven deadly sins of decision making, and you will have the tools to use them to your advantage.

THE SCIENCE OF DECISION MAKING

To understand why we make the seven deadly sins of decision making, we must explore the worlds of cognitive psychology and behavioral economics. Cognitive psychologists call our rational decision-making limitations *bounded rationality.* Our ability to make rational decisions is restricted by the cognitive limitations of our mind, the amount of information we have, the quality of that information, the amount of time we have to make a decision, our emotional state, the biases and fallacies hidden in our unconscious minds, and how our brains are wired to process information. With that many factors influencing our decision making, it is a miracle that we ever make any decisions, much less good ones. Once you understand these limitations, you will learn how to make better decisions more consistently, how to avoid techniques used to influence your decision making, and how to influence the decision making of others.

Our cognitive functioning can be broken down into two processing systems: analytical and auto-pilot. Our *analytical system* is the logical, conscious cognitive processor. It's activated when we have time to pay attention and analyze a situation or problem. Unfortunately, all that analyzing takes time and energy. The healthy, normal human mind is incapable of conducting a thorough analysis for every decision made throughout the day. That "analysis paralysis" would prevent us from leaving the house in the morning. Can you imagine working through the pros and cons of every breakfast choice each morning? What if you performed a cost-benefit analysis for every product you purchased in the grocery store? There simply isn't enough time in our hectic lives to thoroughly analyze every decision, so we develop cognitive shortcuts for problem solving.

These methods for simplifying decision making are called *heuristics* and without them we would go nuts. Think of a heuristic as a cognitive rule of thumb—a way to make a decision quickly and move on to the next decision. Once established, these heuristics are used by our *autopilot system* to make decisions without thorough analysis. Which system do you think is in control most of the time?

In essence, our brains are operating systems designed for speed in an unpredictable and unsafe world. Our ancient ancestors had to think fast because physical threats (invaders and predators) necessitated quick decisions for self-preservation. It didn't pay, survival-wise, to spend too much time analyzing one's options with a large hungry animal bearing down. Our ancestors had to think fast or die young.

When the Emotional Tail Wags the Rational Dog

Autopilot mostly operates unconsciously. It is intuitive and relies primarily on feelings and mental shortcuts to make decisions. On the up side, auto-pilot prevents information overload. The down side of autopilot is that it leaves us susceptible to mistakes driven by biases and fallacies.

A *bias* is a pre-conceived, often unfair, belief or opinion and a *fallacy* is a false belief based on an unsound argument. Pre-conceived notions and false beliefs are the root of poor decision making, and they hide in our unconscious mind, the engine of autopilot cognitive processing. While we need autopilot, we must also acknowledge the blind spots that come with it. To understand these biases and fallacies is to uncover the flaws in our own thinking. Well, at least it's a start.

The famous Swiss psychiatrist Carl Jung once said, ("Thinking) tells us what this thing is; (feeling) tells us what this thing is to us," Jung believed that we experience things unconsciously and, as a result, we are oblivious to the significance of these experiences on our emotions. When triggered, these unconscious memories, and the emotions associated with them, surface to influence our actions and reactions. Therefore, our behavior and decision making is largely driven by emotions buried deep in our unconscious mind.

If you find this concept unbelievable, try this exercise: pick a political or religious topic for which you have a very strong opinion. Now imagine someone with an opposing view of that topic and hold an imaginary debate. Think of the arguments the opposition would use and how you would convince them that you are (obviously) correct.

Does the thought of the encounter bring up any emotions? Do you feel any changes to your physiology? How do you feel about your imaginary opposition? Do you find yourself making assumptions about their overall character based on your difference of opinion? Politics and religion tend to carry emotionally charged belief systems. Just thinking about a hot topic can unearth powerful emotions.

Now, take a deep breath. Find your happy place, and let's move on.

THE FIRST DEADLY SIN

JUSTIFYING: Hearing What We Want to Hear
(And Seeing What We Want to See)

As I was dressing one morning, I made a shocking discovery. An inordinate number of blue shirts hung in my closet. There were different prints and patterns, of course, but almost every shirt was some variation of the color blue. The only exceptions were two lonely white shirts I wore on more formal occasions. I hadn't purposely set out to buy blue shirts exclusively, but I must unconsciously gravitate to the color. Blue is the color of trust and responsibility. Blue is reliable and in control. Blue is steady and dependable. Admittedly, that's how I see myself. Blue is also boring and predictable, which is *not* how I see myself. I shared this revelation with my wife, Kellie;

surprisingly, she wasn't surprised at all. So much for self-awareness.

This will not do, I thought. So, I grabbed most of the blue button-downs from their hangers (not all, because that's just irresponsible) and donated them to a local charity. I then partook in a little retail therapy to replace my boring shirts with exotic, interesting, bold colors, prints, and patterns. Anything but blue and boring. I'll show the world that I'm exciting, adventurous, and unpredictable!

Years have passed since my wardrobe revelation. I recently decided to assess my wardrobe again through a more mature set of eyes. As of the writing of this passage, I have twelve blue shirts hanging in my closet. I also have three white shirts, one dark-purple check, and one pink shirt. I rarely wear the pink shirt. It's just too flashy.

Based on this short description of my wardrobe and personality, you have probably made a few assumptions about me. It's ok; I won't blame you for stereotyping. Some of us are blue shirt guys and I'm ok with that now.

Like the clothing we wear, the automobiles we drive often tell volumes about us. You can probably guess the types of cars that I've owned over the years: Nissans, Hondas, Mazdas, and Toyotas (with a Ford thrown in for good measure). All safe, reliable, practical models.

At the same time that I traded in my blue shirts for a more interesting wardrobe, I decided to break the mold and buy an extravagant new car. My wife and I were both driving Toyota 4-Runners at the time. They were both gray with a gray interior (I know). I had promised myself that I would buy a "fun" car upon my completion of graduate school, but had put the purchase off for a number of years.

One reason was that we simply did not need a new car. Kellie's SUV was eight years old, had given us 150,000 reliable miles, and had never caused a problem in any way. It was a wonderful car. My 4-Runner was a little newer; pre-owned, but in perfect condition.

Another reason: a fun, sporty car simply wasn't a practical investment for our hard-earned money. We had every intention of keeping both SUVs until the wheels fell off. Look, I had gotten all "A's" in finance, accounting, and economics courses, so I knew better than to waste money on a depreciating asset.

Those justifications were in keeping with values that are important to me: hard work, careful financial planning, providing for my children. Those values are central to my *self-identity*. I saw myself, and wanted others to see me, as a person who would put those considerations above indulging in an impractical luxury purchase.

At the same time, I had made that promise to myself because, just as I thought of myself as a person who would wear flashy shirts, in the back of my mind I saw myself as a person who would own an expensive, sporty car. Those images were part of my *ideal self*, the person I wanted to be.

One day, Kellie asked why I hadn't ever purchased the fun car I had promised myself years earlier. I gave her my rationale for the delay, but she reminded me that the new car wasn't an investment, it was a reward.

That changed everything. I deserved a little luxury, because I had worked so hard! It seemed like an excellent reason to buy the sporty, fun car I wanted.

The Magic Word: "Because"

One reason that rationale was so convincing was that it used the magic word: *because*. In 1977 Harvard psychology researcher Ellen Langer conducted one of the most important studies in human decision making: The Copy Machine Study. The study itself seemed rather absurd. Members of Langer's research team attempted to cut in front of people waiting in line to make photocopies. The researcher then said one of three phrases to the innocent bystander in line:

- "Excuse me, I have 5 pages. May I use the Xerox machine?"
- "Excuse me, I have 5 pages. May I use the Xerox machine, because I'm in a rush?"

- "Excuse me, I have 5 pages. May I use the Xerox machine, because I have to make copies?"

This experiment sounds silly, but it was ground breaking. How successful were these statements in influencing compliance? The first statement was the *least* successful. 60% of the people standing in line allowed the researcher to cut in front of them. This number seems surprisingly high to me because there was no compelling reason to allow the researcher in line. It was pure altruism on the part of the bystanders.

Predictably, the second statement was the *most* successful. When researchers added, "Because I'm in a rush," 94% of the people standing in line would allow them to cut in. That is an astoundingly high rate of compliance and a 34-percentage point improvement over the first statement. Providing the person with a justification influenced them to comply with the request.

The most fascinating finding of this study was the result of the third statement: "Excuse me, I have 5 pages. May I use the Xerox machine, because I have to make copies?" This statement included the word *because*, but did not provide a reasonable justification. Everyone in line needed to make copies. Why would the researchers' need to make copies take precedence over anyone else's need to make copies? And yet, this statement garnered compliance 93% of the time.

At face value, the third statement was no more compelling than the first. It provided no real reason to influence compliance. Why would this statement elicit a favorable response at such a high rate? Researchers believe the word "because" triggers a mental short cut or heuristic. It activates our brain's autopilot thinking. The word is used as a precursor to a reason or justification; therefore, our unconscious mind automatically perceives a justification even when there isn't one.

Why is this finding so important? Because Langer's team proved that justification is the key factor in decision making and influence. We need justification in some way, shape, or form, in order to make a decision. And, that justification does not have to be logical, reasonable, or even real.

My wife's assertion that I deserved a reward was compelling for another reason. Justification is vulnerable to *confirmatory bias,* the tendency to favor information that confirms our beliefs. We've all had the experience of making a "gut feeling" decision and then justifying it with analysis tailored to prove we've made the right choice. We are often our own worst enemy because our mind will fight to confirm the justification. It will seek evidence to prove our decision was right and ignore evidence that discredits the justification. In other words, we hear what we want to hear, see what we want to see.

Why do we do this? Because human beings crave *consistency*. It is a primary motivator of our behavior. By contrast, inconsistency is considered to be undesirable. Would you like to be described as erratic, unpredictable, or unstable? You would most likely find it quite insulting, just like the rest of us.

Consistency offers a safe haven for automatic responding because it provides a shortcut decision-making process to deal with our busy modern life. Once we have made a decision (about our values, religion, politics, world views, or bath soap) we no longer need to evaluate all of the new information we receive. We know how to behave in most situations because our desire is to remain consistent with earlier choices and support our self-identity.

Unwittingly, my wife had given me the perfect justification for creating that desired consistency with both my self-identity and with my ideal self: I could have my fun car while remaining true to my values. Because this was a way to resolve that conflict *and* get what I wanted, I had a stronger emotional reaction to this rationale than to the rationales for NOT buying the car, sensible though they may have been. And I did not recognize what had happened, because the allure of consistency led me into an automatic response.

It was one of many times I committed the deadly sin of justification, making myself an easy target for persuasion.

Because I Am a Good Father...

One clear and sunny Saturday of a Memorial Day weekend, my little family of four walked into our local Mercedes-Benz dealership to test drive a car. This was our first planned stop of many that day. I had a long list of other makes and models that I was interested in test-driving. We had no plans to buy a new car that weekend, we just wanted to enjoy the experience of shopping around. Owning a new Mercedes would be fun, but was really more of an aspiration than a reality at that point.

The minute we walked in the showroom door, there it was: a shiny black Mercedes SUV in all its new-car glory. We literally physically bumped into it. I asked my wife if she had ever driven a Mercedes. She had not. I nodded my head at the SUV and said, "Let's take this thing for a test drive. Just for fun." She wasn't all that interested. She loved her eight-year-old Toyota. It had sentimental value. We had driven both of our kids home from the hospital in it. Her 4-Runner was practically part of the family. And we weren't in the market for an SUV, anyway. I was interested in another model.

A friendly salesman appeared out of nowhere. He had overheard our conversation and was eager for us to take the SUV out for a ride. Kellie was reluctant, but I insisted. Why not? We had all day. It's just for fun. We're never going to buy this car. We didn't want another SUV.

The salesman grabbed the keys while I went for the kids' car seats. We all met at the front of the dealership where my family was waiting with that beautiful SUV, sparkling in the sun. With the family loaded in the car, Kellie took the wheel and off we went. A mile down the road, she unexpectedly pulled over. Is something wrong? It looked like she was about to cry.

"I love this car," she said. Oh, boy. I didn't see this coming, but frankly, I loved the car too. And I hadn't even driven it. But I wasn't there for an SUV, I wanted a sporty car. There was no need whatsoever to purchase an expensive, high-end SUV. What a terrible waste of money. We were just having a little fun, right?

When we returned to the dealership, I thanked the salesman for allowing us to take the test drive. He began running through the laundry list of safety features and shared a few anecdotes about the quality and safety standards of the brand. There was no mention of performance or prestige, only safety and quality.

I explained that we were actually there to test drive another vehicle and weren't in the market for an SUV. We then took the car in which I was originally interested out for a test drive. When we returned, the salesman gave us the same pitch as the one for the SUV: safety and quality, quality and safety. Not a word about power, performance, aesthetics, or status. I loved the car as much as I had loved the SUV.

You can probably predict what happened next. By Monday evening, we had two brand-new Mercedes parked in our garage. One black SUV and one blue sporty sedan (mine of course). We didn't even bother going to another dealership or test-driving another car. We also had two new expensive car loans and more than a little buyer's remorse.

What just happened? How did mister blue shirt wind up buying two impractical vehicles in one weekend? In hindsight, the salesman made some accurate assumptions about us from the minute we walked through the door. He knew right away that he didn't have to sell me the cars. He just had to give me permission to buy them.

He knew that we were interested or we wouldn't have asked for a test drive. He also knew that we wanted the cars for their performance and prestige. That's why most people buy luxury brands. Most important, he knew that I really wanted to own a luxury car brand.

His biggest barrier to the sale of those two vehicles was to establish a justification for the purchases. His strategy was to focus on practical decision factors like quality and safety. As a young father, my top concern would be my family. Safety was the perfect justification for me to *act* on my desire to purchase an impractical car (or two).

Another barrier to the sale was price. It may not be flattering, but my motives also included *social comparison*, the prestige of a Mercedes. He cleverly associated prestige with quality: The Mercedes-Benz brand is prestigious because it has a long track record of producing high-quality automobiles. He played on my assumption that quality has a direct relationship with price: you get what you pay for. Price is often perceived as proof of quality.

With quality and safety successfully "proven," my luxury purchase seemed almost practical. I *wanted* those Mercedes, and had probably made the decision to buy them in my unconscious mind before the helpful salesman provided me with the justification. I accepted his reasoning – and down-played my own reasonable concerns about cost and practicality – because doing so gave me permission to act on my desire and justify the decision after the fact.

So, why did I buy those two Mercedes? Because I'm a good father, of course.

The Best and Brightest

I was given this sage advice as a young man: if you want to be successful, do what successful people do. The logic of mirroring the behavior of successful people applies to almost every facet of life: career, finances, relationships, health, and even recreational activities. Successful people have figured things out, so why not learn about decision making from them?

The question is whom should we emulate for their decision-making prowess? Based on the Mercedes story you might leave me off the list (anyone in the market for a previously owned Mercedes?).

We might turn to people with highly successful academic careers. Just getting into a prestigious post-graduate program at a highly respected academic institution requires intelligence, hard work, and a track record of successful decision making.

Located in beautiful Cambridge, Massachusetts, The MIT Sloan School of Management attracts the best and brightest students from around the world. According to their website, a few notable Sloan alumni include a Prime Minister, a former Secretary-General of the UN and several Nobel laureates. The school's alumni have founded more than 650 companies including E*Trade, HubSpot, and Zipcar. It is clearly one of the world's most prestigious business schools. This is a pool of people worth emulating.

Let's take the qualification process a step further. How do the best and the brightest students in the world—students who have been trained in formal decision analysis methods—make one of the most important decisions of their lives: choosing a place to work after grad-school? Remember, top employers recruit students from programs like The MIT Sloan School of Management, so they typically have options. Very good options.

That's exactly what professor Peer Soelberg wanted to know. He taught a decision-making course at The Sloan School of Management. He wanted to know if his students used the decision-making techniques they learned in his class to properly analyze their employment options. In his book, *Sources of Power, How People Make Decisions,* Gary Klein wrote, "Soelberg's course... taught students how to perform the classical decision analysis method we can call the rational choice strategy." With this method, the decision maker follows these steps:

- Identify the list of options.
- Determine the proper way to evaluate these options.
- Weigh the dimensions of evaluation.
- Rate them.
- Choose the options with the highest rating score.

Soelberg assumed, and I'm sure hoped, his former students would use the rational choice approach he taught. What he learned was... they didn't. His students (the best and the brightest, trained in formal decision-making methods) made this big decision based on gut feeling, not rational analysis.

For his research, Soelberg interviewed his former students to learn how they had made this big decision. When a decision theory professor asks how a major decision was made, we are inclined to respond with an answer we think he wants to hear. The students claimed to have made their decision based on a rational choice analysis.

In reality their decisions had been made prior to any formal decision-making analysis. After initial interviews with the students, before they began their analysis, Soelberg predicted which job they would take. This prediction occurred up to three weeks before they announced their final decisions. Soelberg's predictions were correct an astounding 87% of the time.

To satisfy their need to feel as though they had made a rational decision (and probably to please their former professor) the students did perform a systemic choice evaluation. According to Klein, "They selected one other candidate as a comparison, and then tried to show that their favorite was as good as or better than the comparison candidate on each evaluation dimension." That's right, even the best and brightest decided first, then justified their decision with "analysis."

Going for Broke

Not only is justification deadly to choices in the moment, it also influences our ability to recognize our past mistakes and make new decisions accordingly.

The Great Recession officially began in December 2007. At the time, the national unemployment rate was a relatively ideal 5.0% and had been at that level (or below) for the previous 30 months. The Conference Board reported the Consumer Confidence Index (CCI) was a solid 90.6. By March 2009, the CCI would dip all the way down to a miserable 26.9 and by October of that year, the unemployment rate would reach 10%. It is safe to say the bottom fell out of the U.S. economy and still hasn't fully recovered as of the writing of this book.

While this recession was long and painful, it was far from unprecedented. The National Bureau of Economic Research (the official arbiter of U.S. recessions) reported ten recessions between 1948 and 2011. That means in the 59 years leading up to 2007, recessions occurred roughly every six and a half years. True to form, the last recession the United States experienced was in 2001, only six years earlier. What goes up must come down and apparently, the U.S. economy does so fairly regularly. Given the regularity of the economic pendulum, were Americans prepared to weather the storm?

Not by a long shot. According to Federal Reserve Bank of St. Louis (FRED® Economic Data) the personal savings rate in the United States as of December, 2007, was only 3.0%. That 3.0% savings rate is a far cry from the 12.4% rate reported in December, 1970. While these rates fluctuate from month to month, savings rates have been trending down since the 1970's. We simply were not saving for predictable downturns in the economy.

After such a traumatic experience, did we learn our collective lesson from the Great Recession to save money for a rainy day? Nope. In January 2015, the savings rate was only up to 5.5%. In 2013, almost 6 years after the beginning of the Great Recession, Jillian Berman reported this in The Huffington Post: "75% of Americans don't have enough savings to cover their bills for six months."

There is an epidemic of poor financial decision making in the United States. According to the American Savings Education Council in 2014, "only a third of Americans felt prepared for their long-term financial future." According to the Employee Benefit Research Institute, there is a national retirement savings deficit of over $4.13 trillion in the U.S. A 2012 Fidelity Investments study estimated that employees needed eight times their ending salary in order to meet their basic needs in retirement. The average American is nowhere near where he or she needs to be to meet basic retirement thresholds.

In his Market Watch article, "5 Lies People Tell Themselves about Saving for Retirement," Chuck Jaffe analyzes our justifications for continuing unsound financial behavior. They are examples of the *ostrich effect*, where we simply avoid reality by pretending an uncomfortable situation doesn't exist.

The article lists these familiar justifications:

- *I have time to catch up.* Maybe, but catching up might require lifestyle changes such as saving more and spending less. It also assumes consistent, gainful employment and good health. This is an example of the *optimism bias*, which is understating the likelihood of experiencing negative events. It also employs the *valence effect*, where we overstate the likelihood of good things happening to us rather than bad things.
- *I'm planning to die broke.* Planning to outlive your assets is just a shortsighted and bad idea. In addition to being a burden on family, friends, or society, you might decide you don't like living the "broke lifestyle." By the time you retire, it will be too late to recover.
- *No one in our family has ever needed long-term care. When our time comes, we don't linger.* Wishful thinking is not a strategy. What if you're wrong?

- *Investment companies are just trying to scare us into keeping money with them.* Yes, for-profit businesses are there to make a profit and that includes financial advisors. As the client, it is your prerogative to hold them accountable. There are many lower cost investment alternatives like discount brokers.
- *When the time comes, if I don't have enough, I'll adjust.* The best predictor of future behavior is past behavior. If you haven't adjusted your spending and savings habits by now, do you really believe you will change in the future?

So, why won't we save for a rainy day or for the retirement we have worked so hard to enjoy? Just ask. We have our justifications.

There are, of course, other reasons for a lower rate of savings. The personal savings rate is defined as a percentage of disposable personal income. As they recover from the previous financial downturn, households may have less disposable income and therefore feel too pinched to save a higher percentage for the next crisis.

But what about people with high income and plenty of resources to hire qualified financial advisors? Saving shouldn't be a burden for someone with excessive disposable income compared to the average wage earner in the U.S., right?

Let's take professional football and basketball players as an example. According to Forbes, on average, NFL players made $2 million and NBA players made $4.9 million in 2013. These income levels are approximately 39 times higher (NFL) and 96 times higher (NBA) than the median household income in America. To put that into perspective, it would take a typical American family almost 96 years to earn what an average professional basketball player makes in one year. Shouldn't an average NBA player be set for life after only one year in the league?

In 2009, Sports Illustrated estimated that 60% of NBA players are broke within five years of retiring and 78% of NFL players are broke within only two years of leaving the game. In one case, NBA star Allen Iverson, who earned around $200,000,000 in salary and endorsements during his NBA basketball career, is reportedly broke. Reporting on the story in Forbes, James Marshall Crotty said, "It's a sad and shameful denouement for a man who, pound-for-pound on his six foot, 165-pound frame, is the most gifted and fearless guard to ever play pro basketball."

This topic has gotten a great deal of press over the past few years. It supports the "dumb jock" stereotype, but players in both leagues are predominantly drafted out of college. They have at least a little exposure to higher education. NFL players typically have at least three years of college, while basketball players may be drafted after only one year of college or a year out of high school. The

NFL also conducts workshops for rookies covering personal finance. These athletes have the means to hire qualified advisors to devise plans for their long-term financial security. With access to superior resources and education, why do so many pro athletes make such poor financial decisions?

Jones Envy

One reason some professional athletes go broke is that while the money is pouring in, they live the extravagant lifestyle of an exclusive club—other professional athletes. That lifestyle becomes no longer viable after they retire; unfortunately, many are unable to adjust to a reduced income. Giving in to the real pressure to belong and compare favorably in their peer group, they quickly spend all of their money.

If you were a teenager in the early 1980's you will remember the iconic original Members Only jacket. As a product of that era, I distinctly remember when we began to notice the cool set of early adopters wearing this interesting new brand. It was clearly a fad that would fade as quickly as it had appeared. My friends and I dismissed the brand from the outset. Until....

One day, my friend Troy walked into homeroom class wearing a brand-new Members Only jacket, hot off the rack. He flopped heavily into the seat next to mine with the grunt of a greeting teenage boys give to one another. He said nothing of the jacket. My other friend, John, and I looked at each other in disbelief. Troy was in our group. He wasn't one of the popular kids; he was one of us. Who does he think he is?

John and I immediately set about making fun of Troy's newfound fashion sense. Of course, that behavior was just masking our envy. We wanted Members Only jackets because one of our own had a Members Only jacket. Troy played his hand like a poker champion by not defending his new look. He simply giggled at our jibes because he knew he had the upper hand. That stoked our desire to be in the Members Only club.

The very next Monday John walked into homeroom wearing his own Members Only jacket. I was now on the outside looking in. My mother was usually the gatekeeper for the purchase of kids clothing in our house, but I would need to work on my father for this request. This was an expensive purchase and I already had a perfectly good light jacket hanging in the closet. There was no reasonable explanation for my desire to own a Members Only jacket other than the fact that I wanted to be in the club.

My father was a CPA and loved to brag about how cheap he was (believe it or not). This was going to be an uphill battle. I argued my point, but he didn't see the value of making an expensive purchase to replace something that worked perfectly fine. He said, "You're just trying to keep up with the Joneses."

"Who are the Joneses?" I replied.

"It's just an expression," he said. "It means you are too concerned about material possessions."

As it turns out, there really was a family on which that idiom was based. The Joneses of New York were a wealthy family who were connected by marriage to John Mason, the founder of Chemical Bank. The Joneses, along with other wealthy New Yorkers, began building "villas" along the Hudson Valley in the mid-1800's. One such mansion built by Elizabeth Schermerhorn Jones had 24 rooms and looked like a Scottish castle. This pretentious structure spurred the building of other ridiculously large estates along the Hudson by prominent families of New York. Clearly this behavior was an expression of social status through conspicuous consumption.

It was said at the time that only four hundred people in New York really mattered. It was very important for the Jones family to be on *The Four Hundred*, a list of social elites who were invited to Mrs. William Backhouse Astor, Jr.'s famous Patriarchs Ball. These were the members of high society. The Joneses were members of the club.

This was the origin of the phrase "keeping up with the Joneses." Achieving social status through conspicuous consumptions was, is, and will always be an expensive endeavor.

I had to wait until Christmas to receive my Members Only jacket, which seemed like an unbearable amount of time to wait. After the holiday break, I proudly wore my new status symbol to school. When I got off the bus I quickly identified the hottest gift of that year—the Members Only jacket. Everybody was now a member. And just like that, the club wasn't so prestigious. The jackets soon fell out of fashion.

My father was right, of course, but social status is very important to us. Human beings are social animals. My status symbol was on a much smaller scale than the outrageously expensive villas of the Joneses and their ilk, but the principle is the same. It was a ticket into the club. Membership meant acceptance, just like seeing your name on the prestigious list *The Four Hundred*. Something inevitably came along to replace the Members Only jacket as a status symbol, but I can't remember what. Whatever it was, I'm quite certain I wanted it.

We justify many of our behaviors in the name of social status and belonging because that sense of belonging is inherently important to us. Unfortunately, it can also lead to poor choices and deplorable behavior. Keeping up with the Joneses is an alluring treadmill and it's hard to step off.

The Power of Authority

There are two definitions of authority: power and expertise. Both play a role in decision making through justification.

The first definition involves *position power*. Being the boss brings with it inherent advantages with regard to the principle of justification. Because the boss has decision making authority, his or her command is justification for making a decision.

Be aware of your susceptibility to blind obedience of authority figures. You might bear responsibility for following a bad order. The king never orders his own head removed. Blind obedience is for scapegoats and suckers.

The other definition of authority is to be seen as an *expert*. This form of authority also carries the power of influence and does not require a title or position. We rely heavily on expert opinions and trust them to be informed and accurate. How often do you question your dentist or mechanic or lawyer? Their knowledge and experience far exceeds our own in those fields, so we assume competence until proven otherwise. This level of influence also works with friends and acquaintances that have a particular set of expertise. We seek and value their opinion. Experts have a tremendous impact on our decision making.

In both cases, letting a real or perceived authority do our thinking is a way of abdicating the responsibility of decision making. In fact, many people see decision making as a cumbersome undertaking. Paco Underhill supported this belief in his book *Why We Buy*: "Many are outright relieved to let go of the burden of decision making." Therefore, making a decision based on the advice of an authority figure is a powerful and welcome justification.

The Siren's Call

In Greek mythology, the Sirens were beautiful creatures with seductive music that lured sailors to the dangerous, rocky shores of their island. The fate of sailors who followed the Siren's call was calamity: shipwreck and doom. The Siren's song was so attractive that, in Homer's classic poem *The Odyssey*, when Odysseus' ship passed their island he ordered his men to tie him to the mast so he couldn't act on his desire to follow the Siren's song. He then had his crew plug their ears with wax until they passed onto safer waters. Odysseus made a good decision. He and his men passed the Siren's without disaster.

Odysseus knew that his short-term decisions would have long-term consequences. The Sirens' call was exceedingly alluring, but it would eventually lead to catastrophe. This story illustrates the lengths Odysseus was willing to take to avoid making a poor decision driven by our emotional, irrational cognitive processing system.

So how can we resist the Siren's call of justification? I'm not implying you should tie yourself to the mast of a ship to avert temptation (although that did work for Odysseus). But it is important to challenge our own thinking and decision making. We must accept the fact that there are flaws in our thought process that lead to poor decisions. Find confidantes to challenge your rationale on important decisions. Think of them as the side mirrors on your automobile. They help to identify danger hiding in your blind spots. This approach is not easy on the ego, but it is essential to making better decisions.

How can we use this information to avoid becoming the victim of other people's poor decisions and recognize when justification is influencing our own?

On the Flip Side of Justifying

We make decisions for irrational and emotional reasons and then justify them to others and ourselves—everyone does it. Even when we have an understanding of this flawed heuristic, we continue to make decisions emotionally and justify them with seemingly rational reasons.

On the flip side, we can use this knowledge to our advantage. Here are a few ideas to leverage this sin:

Provide justification. We just learned that justification is the key factor in decision making, and that the justification must support the self-identity of the decision maker. The Mercedes salesman wisely played on my identity as a father. My kids were literally sitting in the room while he explained the benefits of owning the cars. Therefore, the justifications he provided were around safety and quality. Those automobile purchases confirmed that I was a good father. And that was all the justification I needed.

In situations where the decision maker is wavering between multiple choices, simply provide them with a justification for the favorable decision. This gives them permission to make the decision.

Promote consistency. We like to exhibit behaviors that appear to confirm our beliefs. The more deeply held the belief, the more powerful the need to behave consistently in support of that belief. Offer a justification that supports the decision maker's desire for consistency with their self-identity. This is an extremely effective tactic. Here are some examples:

- "I know that you will tell the truth *because* you are such an honest person."
- "I know that you will complete the task *because* you have always been a dependable person."
- "I am sure that you will back my promotion *because* you have been so supportive of my career."
- "I know that you will buy a car with a proven safety record *because* you are such a good father."

Statements like these hit right at the heart of self-identification and make us all extremely vulnerable to influence. We will always try to do what we perceive to be the "right thing" in support of our belief system, even if that thing isn't necessarily good or right. It only has to be consistent with how we see ourselves. This is why we find compliments so alluring. They confirm how we see ourselves or, at least, how we would like others to see us.

Say the magic word. The examples above also use the magic word: *because*. Justifying is a cognitive blind spot and therefore a powerful tool of influence, and we are all susceptible to it *because* that is how our brains work. Even a shaky justification can get a turbo boost with this sentence structure: Desired choice + because + justification supporting consistency and confirming self-identity.

Set expectations. Expectations are powerful influencers. Because of our craving for consistency, when we believe beforehand that something will be good, we will look for reasons that justify that expectation. If you tell someone upfront that something is distasteful, the odds are good that they will end up agreeing with you—not because their experiences tell them so, but because of their expectations.

Offer justifications that support the expectations you set. And remember to use the word "because." For instance, if you set high expectations for a restaurant, point out aspects of the restaurant that justify the expectation: this place is great *because of* the beautiful décor, the friendly staff, the distinctive tableware, and the interesting menu choices. Use whichever elements best support your suggestion. If your companions can justify the expectations, they will remember the experience favorably.

Here is another example directed at a new boss: "I've heard that you are a wonderful leader *because* you take such good care of your team." You might throw in something about compensation or autonomy or guidance or whatever it is you seek from your new boss. Set expectations for the behavior or decisions you desire. The power of suggestion is time tested.

Form a "members only" club. Social acceptance is important to us. It's why we buy expensive villas and trendy jackets. We want to be in the club, whatever club that might be. A very powerful message to hear is: You are one of *us* because you (insert behavior, interest, trait, or ideology here). It is simply peer pressure and we all fall for it to a certain extent.

The club you leverage must support the self-identity or ideal self of the decision maker. It should be a group in which you both already belong: political, religious, professional, social status, or even a character trait (e.g. honest, hard-working, responsible). People will do all sorts of irrational things to become a member of or prove they belong in the club.

Compare and contrast. The justification process relies on comparison. We constantly compare ourselves to other human beings—usually to people in our peer group. Use comparison to influence decision making. Find favorable or unfavorable examples to compare and contrast the decision maker in support of the desired behavior, or point out when someone behaves out of character or makes a decision that does not support their self-identity.

For example, a better approach for my father to convince me not to bother with the Member's Only jacket would have been something like: "You are such an independent, a nonconformist. Why would you want to look like *them*?" As a teenager, I didn't identify with the trend-setting kids. I didn't like them. I saw myself as unique and enjoyed expressing my individuality. Comparing me to the group that I did not wish to belong would have been a powerful persuasion technique.

Provide the decision maker with choices. We typically won't go outside the consideration set of choices to make a decision. We choose between the options set before us. Three options are ideal in most situations and they must be easy to compare. The key differentiating factor between comparable items is what will be used to justify the decision. Be strategic when offering choices and be sure to make the key differentiating factor obvious and easy to compare.

Price is often a default key decision factor. This is the basis of the "good, better, best" pricing structure that retailers often use. Each step up the pricing ladder seems to be a slightly better value for the consumer. The goal for the retailer, of course, is to persuade people to buy higher priced merchandise than they intended because the higher priced items seem to offer a better value compared to products at the other price points.

Shoppers can also be enticed to spend more than originally budgeted by a price-multiple offer, multiple items offered at a discount rather than single items at the full retail price. This technique works because the price for the sale product is easy to compare to the retail ticket price. That is why *both* the original price and the sales price are listed on the price tag—to give the consumer a point of comparison. Compared to the original price, the sale price looks to be great value.

Be seen as an authority. Remember the two definitions of authority: expertise and position power. Make known and leverage your expertise to influence the decisions of others. If you are not in a position of power, assume one through association. Two options are to become the gatekeeper for a person with position power or become the leader of an important project. You will be amazed at the influence that comes from assuming informal position power. Whether real or imagined, power and expertise are compelling because we tend to feel a sense of duty to obey authority.

• • • • •

MOMENTARY LAPSE OF REASON:
Autopilot

Autopilot is an unconscious thought process that allows us to get through the myriad of low-importance, trivial decisions. Autopilot is great when we're grocery shopping, but we also tend to go on autopilot when we most need our wits about us. We become extremely vulnerable to influence and, in a *momentary lapse of reason*, make snap judgments we later regret.

Our mission is to avoid these lapses of reason by recognizing when we are on autopilot in situations that require a deliberate thought processes. These tend to be moments of stress such as when we have too little information, too much information, emotional arousal, time pressure, or fear. We will cover these situations in more depth in these *Momentary Lapses of Reason* sections.

We also want to recognize when others are in autopilot mode and making poor decisions. The techniques in this book will show you how to influence the decision maker to make better choices. Finally, we want to identify when others are taking advantage of our autopilot thinking to influence our decisions.

• • • • •

Kenneth J. Taylor

THE SECOND DEADLY SIN

STEREOTYPING: Judging a Book by its Cover

Who's the Boss?

As a sophomore in college I decided to find a summer internship in what I believed to be my chosen field, advertising. At that point, I hadn't officially declared a major, so it made sense to get a little real-world experience before making such a significant decision about my future. The most exciting opportunity was with Turner Advertising, an in-house agency at Turner Broadcasting System.

I walked into the Turner offices overflowing with confidence. I wore my brand-new interview clothes, fresh off the rack, and carried a brown pleather folder containing exactly three resumes and a pad of yellow paper. The resumes thoroughly explained my work experience as a bag boy for a small grocery store in high school and as a bus boy for a Mexican restaurant in college.

I interviewed with a very serious woman named Cindy, who led the account management team. Her office was sparse to say the least; it had very few decorations of any kind. She didn't smile at all during our encounter. I was quite intimidated.

I handed her my resume, which she didn't bother to read. She sat behind her desk and looked me up and down. She didn't say a word for what seemed like an eternity. I began to sweat in my new sport coat.

Then Cindy asked me a series of questions, but I was so frightened I can't remember a single one. Nor am I sure what I said, but whatever I said worked. When she finished asking questions she looked me up and down again and said, "Okay kid. We'll hire you for the summer."

Then it was revealed that they would pay me $5 an hour. I believe my response was, "Wow, I get to work here and you're going to pay me too?" I think I also said the word "awesome" once or twice, but again, it was all a blur.

This was a time before electronic communications were ubiquitous. There was no email. People didn't carry mobile phones. When notes needed to be sent or advertising materials needed client approval, couriers or interns physically delivered them. I had two key responsibilities: deliver items all over the complex and attend meetings with one of the five women in the group. As a result, I interacted with almost every business Ted Turner owned at the time and met innumerable fascinating people.

The only downside to the job, if any, was almost all of the people I interacted with were at least a decade older and in a completely different stage of life. In meetings, I often felt like the little brother tagging along.

One morning I was invited to a meeting at the Techwood campus in midtown Atlanta. After a few minutes wandering the hallways I found the right room, a large space with a thick, heavy wooden table in the center surrounded by cushy chairs. There was nothing on the walls. To the left was a small serving table with coffee and a plate of pastries. My boss had not yet arrived.

Five executives were chatting near the table; when I entered the room, their conversation ceased for a moment. They looked me over, determined I was harmless, and resumed their conversation. I immediately felt out of place.

I made my way to the snack table, grabbed a Danish and poured a cup of coffee. Soon after, a young man, who didn't appear to be much older than me, burst through the door and made a beeline for the snack table. I was relieved to find someone close to my age, so I struck up a conversation with something like, "Hey, what's up?"

His name was Scott. He was a short, high-energy guy. He wore a nice suit, had a confident swagger, and didn't seem intimidated by the more experienced people in the room. I assumed he was an assistant or direct report to one of the executives standing nearby. We had a short, friendly conversation about our favorite television shows. I then asked what the meeting was about, but before he could answer, a tall woman in a light-colored pantsuit looked our way and said, "Is everyone here?"

Just then my account executive boss walked into the room and Scott said to me, "I think that's everyone. Excuse me." He then walked to the head of the table and called the meeting to order. The older executive types quickly and obediently took their seats. My jaw dropped. It had never crossed my mind that this young man was in charge.

I learned later that Scott was Scott Sassa. He was in fact a big wig at Turner and later became a very powerful person in broadcast entertainment. Because he was young and took the time to converse with me, a lowly intern, I made the assumption that he must be in a lower-level position with the company. He was young for an executive, but that didn't mean he wasn't capable or even excellent at his job. I was guilty of judging a book by its cover.

Stereotyping is an example of an exception fallacy, in which data about one member of a group is used to draw conclusions about the entire group. It is a fallacy of generalization. When we stereotype, we assume the person has a set of beliefs and behavioral characteristics based on their group classification. I was young and held a lower position in the company. Scott Sassa was also young, and I mistakenly assumed he was like me in other ways. Under ordinary circumstances, speaking so informally to a higher-up would have been a very poor decision. Luckily for me, there is nothing ordinary about Scott Sassa.

The truth is we all stereotype. We always have and we always will. No one with a normal functioning human brain is exempt. It is how our brains are wired. To combat the influence of stereotyping in our own lives, we must accept that our cognitive processing is imperfect and strive to better understand this thought process.

It is widely believed that stereotyping is inherently mean-spirited or bad; certainly, history books are filled with stories of unconscionable behavior as a result of biases associated with this line of thinking. But in reality, stereotyping itself is just a cognitive shortcut, a form of autopilot thinking. It's a simplification process that allows us to reduce the amount of analysis we have to do in a new situation. Stereotyping is mostly done uncon-sciously and helps us deal with the complicated world in which we live.

Stereotyping is often initiated under time pressure, one of the five triggers of autopilot thinking. Time pressure is the enemy of controlled responding, the ability to respond to a situation based on the rigorous analysis of sufficient information. Controlled responding not only requires time and information, but we must also want to perform the analysis and have the capability to do so. Therein lies the problem.

We often think of stereotypes when applied to race and gender in the United States, but we stereotype people based on any way they can be categorized: political beliefs, religious beliefs, education, comparative wealth, vocabulary, accent, wardrobe, height, weight, age, attractiveness, place of origin, car, house, pet preference, and even sports team affiliation. What set of characteristics do you attribute to a Republican or Democrat? What about an atheist or evangelical? What about a southerner or a cat person or a Philadelphia Phillies fan? You most likely have an extensive list of assumptions about how these people think and behave outside of the attributes of the category in which they are affiliated.

Who's the Boss? (Part 2)

A decade and a half after mistaking Scott Sassa for an entry-level employee, I attended a conference with several of my colleagues. I was in my mid-thirties by this time. My colleagues were about the same age and in the same life stage: young husbands, fathers, homeowners, and middle-managers. We had a great deal in common and enjoyed hanging out together. My boss once called us "the fraternity."

The main purpose for attending the conference was to meet with a number of vendors and customers. Many of our meetings were with people we had only communicated with through email or over the phone. Prior to the conference, we had no idea what many of these people looked like.

At one slow point at the conference, we "frat boys" were huddled in a small group talking when a man broke through our circle and made a beeline to Phil, one of the members of our group. Phil was right out of central casting for a middle-manager corporate-type. He had a round face, strong jaw, a deep commanding voice, and a conservative parted-to-the-side businessman haircut. He always had the shadow of a thick beard that he couldn't tame. His body was a little stocky and he wore very traditional, understated clothing, which fit his outward demeanor. The look on his face was serious and sober, but this was just a show for people outside the fraternity. He was the craziest guy in the group.

In contrast to Phil, I had a baby face and slender build. My features were relatively soft and my jaw pointy. I kept my wavy hair cut short because it looked unkempt when I grew it longer. It was a business conference, so I wore conservative clothes, but admittedly I looked like I was wearing my father's wardrobe. Not exactly the look of a leader, but I was in fact running a successful little portfolio of products.

When the gentleman, I'll call him Mr. Daniels, broke our conversation circle he referred to Phil as "Mr. Taylor." He was obviously looking for me. Someone had pointed him in the direction of our assemblage, but didn't specify who I was. He assumed Phil was the guy in charge because Phil looked like a guy who should be in charge.

The other guys shot me a knowing smile as if to say, "I can't believe this is happening." I just shrugged my shoulders. This scenario happened to me all the time and I was curious to see how it played out. Daniels began a long monologue and Phil politely listened, waiting for a break to straighten out the situation.

When the man finally took a breath, Phil gestured his hand at me and said, "Sir, I believe you're looking for Mr. Taylor." Daniels shot me a confusing glance. He looked me up and down. Then without apologizing to anyone, turned his body toward me and repeated the same monologue he had just recited to Phil.

The fraternity had a laugh over it later, but it bothered me. Similar scenarios occurred through-out my career. There are definitely advantages to having a baby face, but it can also become an impediment in business situations when I need to be seen as an authority figure. It's a matter of credibility. Some people look the part and some people don't. As you will see looking the part has an impact on both perceptions and behavior.

The Dr. Fox Effect

In the early 1970's, three psychiatry professors conducted an experiment to determine if the student ratings of a course were influenced more by the personality of the educator than by the educational content. They organized three separate lectures to be held at a continuing education training retreat. The lecture was titled, *Mathematical game theory and its application to physician education (basics/education)*. Those in attendance included professional psychiatrists, psychologists, social workers, and educational administrators.

As educators, they wanted to determine if charismatic teachers and professors could "seduce" students into giving higher evaluation scores. This was and is still important to educators because the student evaluation of teachers (SET) is often used as an official performance assessment. SET results can affect employment factors such as budget allocations, salaries, and even hiring decisions.

The professors hired an actor to give the lectures for this experiment. The man knew absolutely nothing about game theory, so they coached him on the topic just enough to get through the lecture. More importantly, they instructed him to convey irrelevant, conflicting, and meaningless content to these professional educators and administrators.

The first panel of attendees saw the lecture live and the other two groups saw a video of the live lecture. After each session, the attendees were asked to fill out an evaluation of the speaker. How do you think the attendees rated this double-talking, yet charismatic actor?

According to the Journal of Medical Education, the researchers concluded that their hypothesis was supported because 55 lecture attendees responded favorably on a questionnaire about their attitudes toward the lecture. In fact, their positive response was at "the significant level," meaning they really liked it. In essence, the study confirmed the idea that educators' effectiveness should be evaluated using other methods than merely student satisfaction, because students may be heavily influenced by the delivery of the instructor rather than the content of the lecture. They also offered the possibility of using actors to give lectures in the future, citing this may be a more innovative approach to education.

What is fascinating is that 55 highly educated professionals, many of whom were authorities on the subject of game theory, believed this individual was an expert on the topic. How was it so easy to dupe them? I encourage you to watch the *Dr. Fox Lecture* video for yourself on YouTube.

Here's how the actor fooled them. First, the professors selected an actor who looked distinguished and could present the material like an authority. They leveraged the representative heuristic, which is when we estimate the likelihood of a behavior based on how closely a person represents a prototype in our mind. Basically, the actor looked the part. He looked like the stereotypical psych lecturer. He also sounded the part. The actor spoke with ease and confidence even when asked specific questions from the audience. These were questions of which he had no understanding; he just made up answers on the spot.

Second, they used the *perceptual contrast principle*, which is when our minds accentuate the difference between two items presented one after another. In the video, the expert who introduced the phony speaker wore very casual clothing: shorts and sandals. They were on a retreat. The actor wore a suit and tie. He also wore glasses, which gave him an intellectual appearance. Many members of the audience were also more casually dressed than the presenter; by comparison, the actor looked like an authority figure.

Third, they employed the concept of social proof by introducing him with the title, "Dr. Myron L. Fox, an authority on the application of mathematics to human behavior." They even wrote an impressive, but fictitious, curriculum vitae. The people with position authority, the folks in charge of the lecture, established the "fact" that Dr. Fox was an authority on the subject. As a result, the people in the room, some of whom were experts on the topic presented, didn't question the validity of the speaker. Social proof was established. Everyone was on board.

The Dr. Fox experiment taught us something beyond the fact that students will rate charismatic speakers or teachers higher on evaluations. It taught us how easily we are duped. Simply looking or sounding the part is often enough to sway us into believing someone is who we think they are.

In her book, *Survival of the Prettiest*, Dr. Nancy Etcoff described a study conducted by John Marshall Townsend and Gary Levy, in which women were asked to review photographs of four men. Some women saw pictures of "Tom" and "Harry" wearing Burger King uniforms, while "Jim" and "Dan" wore business suits and nice watches. Other women saw pictures of Tom and Harry wearing business suits, while Jim and Dan wore Burger King uniforms. All of the women surveyed were asked which men the women were willing to date, have sex with, or marry. As it turned out, women were not willing to engage in any of those activities with the men wearing Burger King outfits, but they were interested in the same models when they were wearing suits and nice watches. We hate to admit it, but status symbols have meaning. They provide clues to the observer as to the roles we play in life. The old adage rings true: "clothes make the man."

This may be the single most important thing you will take away from this book. Human beings judge each other based on appearances. And, very often, our judgments are wrong.

What Does Strength Look Like?

Frogmen were the predecessors to the prestigious Special Forces unit, the U.S. Navy SEALs. The military called them UDTs or Underwater Demolition Teams. They were in existence from 1943 until 1983 when replaced by the SEAL Team. UDTs were responsible for providing reconnaissance and destroying enemy defensive obstacles on beaches prior to beach landings in combat situations. These men were some of the bravest and most highly skilled military special forces in the world.

Due to the demands of the job, the Frogman selection process was particularly demanding.

Candidates were required to pass an intense 16-week UDT training course, which concluded with Hell Week—six days of unthinkable challenges with little more than two hours of sleep per night. In his book, *The Rogue Warrior*, Richard Marcinko shared his experiences in training to become a Frogman. The regimen included running on beaches while carrying large logs over one's heads; carrying inflatable boats to waterways, paddling across, then carrying them to other waterways to paddle again and repeating the process for eight or ten miles; traversing obstacle courses; and, of course, swimming in every conceivable situation (night, day, warm weather, cold weather, etc.). According to Marcinko, by the end of the 16 weeks, seven out of ten candidates had quit. Those who became Frogmen were among the toughest guys in the United States Navy.

Marcinko came away from this agonizing training with more than his new designation as Frogman, he learned a valuable life lesson as well. He said, "As I looked around at those of us who'd survived, I realized something I'd carry with me for life. It was a simple truth, but a good one: never stereotype anyone. Never assume just by looking that someone is suited for anything."

Marcinko was a big athletic guy, but his swimming buddy had a slight, less-intimidating build. He explained that these Special Forces soldiers come in all shapes and sizes, but "under combat conditions... they are all equally deadly."

We all make these superficial snap judgments about others. Assumptions are made using just a few facts, often based on appearance. Our unconscious mind finds patterns in situations and behavior based on very narrow slices of experience. Some people refer to this as thin-slicing. Unfortunately, thin-slicing is a particularly vulnerable representative heuristic.

When his Special Forces training began, Marcinko assumed the big athletic guys in the group were better suited to survive the intense mental and physical demands required of Frogmen. That particular physical image represented his prototype of an elite Special Forces soldier. He eventually learned that his stereotype led to false assumptions about the worthiness of his fellow candidates.

What Does an American Look Like?

Benjamin Franklin understood the importance of appearances and leveraged that knowledge to his advantage. In *Benjamin Franklin, An American Life*, Walter Isaacson wrote, "Franklin cared about such appearances. American individualists sometimes boast of not worrying about what others think of them. Franklin, more typically, nurtured his reputation, as a matter of both pride and utility, and he became the country's first unabashed public relations expert."

As a printer, Franklin was a tradesman and small business owner. Because he competed against other local printers in Philadelphia, he skillfully differentiated himself from his competition. Ben personally believed in the virtues of hard work, frugality, and industriousness, so he demonstrated these behaviors publicly, both to promote the virtues and to build his personal and professional brand. Even after he was an established printer and successful businessman, he could be seen personally hauling rolls of paper through the streets of Philadelphia to his printer shop instead of asking an employee to manage the menial task.

By the time Franklin arrived in Paris in December of 1776, he was an international celebrity. At the age of 70, he was known as an accomplished writer, scientist, philosopher, statesman, and symbol of liberty. But on this trip, Franklin had something to sell: America. He was in Paris to secure the aid of France in the American Revolution. Parisians gathered along the streets to see this famous man enter the city.

To accentuate the perceived ideals of the great American frontier, he dressed plainly and resisted the fashion of the day, a powdered wig. Instead he wore a soft marten-fur cap... which he had purchased in Canada. The irony, of course, was that he wasn't a frontiersman. He was merely playing the part of a wise and noble backwoods philosopher to impress the Parisians. In fact, Franklin was born in Boston and moved to Philadelphia as a young man. He was a city-dweller. He would have looked just as odd wearing that fur cap on the streets of Philadelphia as he did on the streets of Paris, but he understood the power of looking the part.

How do we avoid deadly sin of stereotyping in our own decision making? The first step is to question how we think of others. Stereotyping occurs most often when we meet someone for the first time, so a good exercise is to question any automatic assumptions you make about someone when you meet him or her. Ask yourself why you came to certain conclusions. I believe this self-analysis is an important step in bringing unconscious beliefs to the surface. If you practice this consistently, you will begin to notice your own biases toward certain groups and you might find that you have judged people unfairly as a result. Awareness is always the first step.

Step two is forgiveness. These biases live in your unconscious mind and have developed through years of subtle conditioning or programming. You have them because you are a human being. Raising these thoughts to your consciousness helps to re-program your thinking for clearer assessments and better decisions.

On the Flip Side of Stereotyping

We are constantly judged based on both physical characteristics and the groups in which we have an affiliation. We can use this knowledge to level the playing field by influencing the judgment and decision making of others. Here are a few techniques to consider:

Look the part. Believe it or not, your business colleagues and clients predict your earning potential and position at first sight, so as Ben Franklin taught us, it is essential to look the part you wish to play. It may seem shallow or vain to be concerned with your appearances, but it is actually a matter of practicality. Not only do we attribute positive traits to attractive people, they also get paid more than less-attractive people by a whopping 12%-14%. Conversely, unattractive people are often assigned negative traits and face discrimination as a result. This is why being perceived as attractive provides an inherent advantage in life. Before we judge employers too harshly, we must keep in mind that the prejudice of beauty functions on an unconscious level. We are all susceptible. This phenomenon is largely attributed to the halo effect, which is when one attribute influences how we perceive other traits or qualities.

The good news is, we do have some control over our appearances. At the conclusion of my graduate studies, one of my professors gave us some unusual advice (at least I thought so at the time). She said, "Always be seen in a suit jacket or at the very least a sport coat." It was a random thought, but she seemed adamant about it. So, I gave it a try. At that point, I had a handful of sport coats and suit jackets that I only wore on special occasions. I began to wear them to work and I noticed a difference right away. People treat you differently when you dress at the higher end of your accepted professional fashion range.

On one occasion a gentleman with whom I had only met a few times offered me a job, unsolicited. He actually said he appreciated that I always wore a sport coat or jacket. Another time, I was surprisingly upgraded on a flight. As I checked in at the gate counter, the airline employee said she was upgrading me because I was the only person on the flight wearing a sport coat.

Dress in a manner that supports how you want to be perceived. If you are looking to elevate your status with any group, the key is to look as if you care about your appearance. A messy look implies a lack of self-respect. If you don't respect yourself, others won't respect you either. This doesn't mean a mechanic should wear a tuxedo. Wear clothing consistent with your profession or group, but it should be at the high end of the fashion range.

More than 200 years ago, Ben Franklin understood the power of looking the part and used it to his advantage throughout his life—first as a publisher in Philadelphia and then as a "frontiersman/statesman" in Paris. Whether you want to be perceived as a doctor, a lawyer, a poet, a pirate, a pawn, or a king... dress the part. Your "audience" expects it.

Nail first impressions. First impressions set anchors in the minds of those we meet. An anchor is a starting point. When an anchor is set, we are biased toward that initial value. Remember, people thin-slice us based on very little information and it's difficult to move them from that first impression. So, the next time you meet someone remember to focus on making a good first impression. You never know who they might turn out to be.

Marshall McLuhan famously said, "The medium is the message," which means the vehicle delivering the content influences the meaning of the message. In this context, the vehicle or medium is you... or at least your appearance and body language.

Body language is an important aspect of one's appearance. I became interested in the topic of body language, or nonverbal communication, years ago, when I noticed an interesting phenomenon occur in business meetings. I worked for a large corporation at the time. One colleague, I'll call him Tim, would offer a smart idea to the group, but it would go unnoticed or outright rejected. Later in the meeting another colleague, I'll call him Tad, would repeat Tim's idea and it would be well received by the same group. This wasn't a one-time occurrence. I noticed it in different settings and with different players. That's when I realized it wasn't the content, but the person delivering the content that truly mattered. I embarked on a research journey to better understand the medium versus message effect. My studies led me to the topic of body language.

I was a bit skeptical about what I learned, so I decided to test some of the key tactics in the real world. I chose the most intense first impression setting possible: the job interview. At that point in my career, I was interviewing with a several different companies. Each company had me interview with a number of people and as you would expect, they all had different personalities and perspectives. It was a great way to test the general principles of body language with a diverse collection of people.

What did I learn? Nonverbal communication is the key to effective face-to-face interaction. In fact, the better my body language, and the less I talked, the more the interviewers liked me. This seems counterintuitive in an interview, but it is true. In general, people care less about what you have to say and more about what they have to say. The interviewers had judged me the second they first saw me. After that, they were looking and listening to validate their initial impression of me. Therefore, I let my clothing and body language do the talking. I asked the interviewers questions and let them talk and talk and talk. In fact, most (not many, most) of my interviewers apologized for not "letting" me do more of the talking.

Was my body language approach effective? Absolutely. I received multiple offers and wound up taking one of the best jobs of my career. In addition to looking the part, the best advice I can give about first impressions is to speak less and listen more. And, always exhibit positive, confident body language.

There are many subtle tactics to body language and I encourage you to learn more about it for yourself. Keep in mind that some body language experts give contradictory advice, so figure out what works for you and forget the rest. I highly recommend Allan and Barbara Pease's book, *The Definitive Book of Body Language*. Below I've paraphrased a few general tips from the book and included a few comments of my own.

- *Smile.* Show your teeth. It's a submissive gesture that puts people at ease and suggests happiness. We generally like happiness, which is why smiling is contagious. Bear in mind, the frequency of smiling depends on cultural norms. For example, people in the

Northeast smile less than people in the South. Flash your pearly whites. Make smiling a part of your facial expression repertoire, but adjust frequency depending on your audience.

- *Nod three times when someone makes a comment.* This confirms to the speaker that you are actively listening and is an indication of interest. Be sure to nod slowly; nodding too fast suggests you want the speaker to finish talking.
- *Display open body language.* Exposing your neck and front torso is a sign of confidence. These are vulnerable areas of the body as they house your vital organs. You'll notice that when people are frightened, they will lower their chin (look downward) and display a closed stance (folded arms or legs protecting vital organs). A closed stance is an unconscious reaction to block a threat. It is akin to a child hiding behind a barrier like a piece of furniture. Another version of the closed stance is hiding your hands in your pockets. This gesture tells others that you are not interested in speaking with them. Generally speaking, display an open stance with chin up to project confidence.
- *Make eye contact* (especially when shaking hands). The eyes are the windows to your soul. They can be the most revealing area of nonverbal communication on the body. There

are too many nuances of eye contact behavior to cover here, but as a general rule, make eye contact with the speaker slightly more than they do with you. If you can identify the speaker's pupil dilation during the course of a conversation, you have made enough eye contact. But beware: if you stare at someone too long, you'll look like a creep. A good rule of thumb is to remove your gaze about a second after the speaker looks away from you, which is a form of mirroring.

- *Mirror the speaker.* Subtly adopt their body language. It makes the speaker feel at ease. Mirroring is an effective tactic to build rapport and we often do it unconsciously. This behavior conveys a feeling of similarity and we typically like people who are like us. Mirroring encompasses things like body position, hand gestures, speed and cadence of speech, and use of vocabulary. The key is subtlety. Don't mimic the speaker like a child. Begin with adopting a similar body position and speech pattern and introduce other like behaviors when they feel natural. You may test your rapport with others by introducing a new gesture or stance to the conversation and observing if they unconsciously adopt it.

Be seen in good company. According to the wisdom of King Solomon, "He that walketh with wise men shall be wise, but a companion of fools shall be destroyed" (Proverbs 13:20). A little heavy handed, but you get the point. Be seen with people who elevate your status or build your credibility.

On the other hand, avoid people who diminish your status and credibility. When I played with kids my mother didn't particularly like, she used to remind me, "You are guilty by association." Not that we did anything wrong, but when something did go wrong... all eyes were on the usual suspects. Being associated with good or bad people affects how others perceive us. Associations are powerful. Choose them carefully and leverage them often.

The same principle works when delivering good or bad news. In his book, *The 48 Laws of Power*, Robert Greene advises us to avoid being the bearer of bad news (Law 24: Play the Perfect Courtier). Negativity sticks to us like a pungent odor. Avoid it at all costs.

Beware: surrounding yourself with successful people does have a downside. While being in good company can help to elevate your status in the eyes of others, it can be deflating for you. Our nature is to compare ourselves to others and it is difficult to turn that thinking off. Constantly feeling as if you are the least (successful, attractive, etc.) in a group will take its toll on your self-esteem.

Be comparably better than those immediately around you. In balance with the general rule to be seen in good company, there are times to leverage the contrast principle with the company you keep. People constantly compare themselves with others. They also compare individuals in a group with other members of the group. Differences are seen as more drastic when they are compared one after another. If you want to make a good impression, position yourself next to someone to whom you compare favorably. Not only can leveraging the contrast principle create a favorable impression with others, this strategy can boost your self-esteem as well.

This principle works especially well if you happen to be in a group that carries widely held misconceptions. When the bar is low in the minds of those who will judge you, exceed expectations in the areas of their greatest bias. You don't have to be the best at something, you only need to outshine expectations. Be the exception to the rule. Do it consistently and without fanfare. Outliers get noticed.

•••••

MOMENTARY LAPSE OF REASON:

Too Little Information

Having too little information is one of five triggers that throw us into our irrational and non-analytical autopilot thinking. Often, when we have too little information or too little experience with something, we defer to someone we believe has more knowledge about the topic. Unfortunately, when we defer to someone else's judgment or expertise we are at the mercy of the biases and fallacies that influence their decision making. Or worse, relying on someone else's opinion makes us susceptible to influence practitioners who want to affect our decisions.

The solution to this problem is simple. You could better inform yourself or, if there isn't the time or desire to learn more about a topic, seek the opinion of multiple experts and triangulate the answer. This approach helps to weed out the biases held by any single expert.

There is, however, a far more insidious problem with autopilot thinking triggered by having too little information. Autopilot is where biases, fallacies, and poor decisions lurk. When we meet someone for the first time, we make assumptions about them based on appearances because that's all we have to go on. We stereotype them. These snap judgments are typically made based on a single attribute, trait, or piece of information, and they lead us to form an opinion about someone's character, likeability, or competence. Even when we receive additional information about that person, the initial impression tends to stick.

How do we avoid the pitfalls of stereotyping due to autopilot thinking? Question your assumptions. Our brains are wired to make snap decisions and judgments. We can't turn that feature off, but we can become more aware of it. When you meet someone for the first time, pay attention to your assumptions about them. When you find yourself "sizing someone up," or "going with your gut," recognize that you are actually using unconscious associations and biases. And those associations and biases are full of mistakes.

Again, we can't stop our minds from activating autopilot, but we can question our assumptions and think before we speak when we have too little information.

THE THIRD DEADLY SIN

FALSE-CAUSE: The Causation
and Correlation Trap

As a kid growing up on the west coast of Florida, I often heard the adults complain about "snowbird" drivers, Midwesterners who had settled in the west coast of Florida to escape the snow up north. They were easily identifiable in traffic by their license plates from states like Michigan and Ohio. The snowbirds drove painfully slowly, even in the passing lane. They would often drive side by side, blocking any attempt to pass, clogging traffic for miles behind them on the interstate, and annoying the hell out of the natives.

Why don't Midwesterners know how to drive? Some time later, I realized that their common place of origin had little to do with their driving skills. The culprit was another commonality: age. These drivers tended to be retirees. Senior citizens typically have diminished eyesight, hearing, and reaction times; therefore, they compensate by driving more cautiously (thankfully). We natives had fallen for the causation and correlation trap.

Human beings look for relationships to explain events and behavior. We strive to understand what causes things to happen so we can try to influence actions and outcomes. Problems occur when we misdiagnose the relationships between causes and effects.

False cause is the mistaken belief that when two events happen at the same time (*correlation*) one event has caused the other (*causation*). Like justification, we are all guilty of assigning false cause because it is driven by autopilot thinking, leading to biases that negatively influence our decision making. In terms of everyday choices, all you need to know about correlation you learned in middle school: *correlation does not imply causation.*

One common example of false cause is the belief in superstitions, such as those prevalent in the world of sports. Both players and fans often believe that a lucky shirt, hat, or pair of underwear can cause a positive event. Some athletes perform rituals before an event, "for luck." As a young baseball player, I never stepped on the baseline when walking on or off the baseball field because stepping on the line was considered bad luck. I certainly didn't want to be on the hook for my team's misfortune, so I avoided the line at all costs.

Many ancient cultures practiced the ritual of human sacrifice to "please the gods" for the benefit of the society: wars, rain, fertility, etc. This practice seems absurd to us today, but certain societies believed in the relationship between sacrificing human beings or animals and positive outcomes for the community. This belief is associated with *conjunction fallacy*, which is the belief that two events are more likely to occur together than one of those events occurring alone. How can we have rain without some sort of sacrifice?

It is the belief in an *association* that holds the power. The connection functions like a *placebo*, a "fake" treatment that plays on our expectations. Studies have shown that the more strongly a person expects the placebo to produce a positive outcome, the more likely it is that person will experience positive results.

Placebos are an example of *spurious correlation*, in which results are assumed to be caused by a correlation of two variables, but are actually related to a third variable. Human sacrifices do not cause rain, just as placebos do not cause positive health results. There may be a correlation, but not causation. For a better understanding of spurious correlations, visit www.tylervigen.com for interesting examples. Here are a few gems I found on the site in July 2015:

- Number of people who drowned by falling into a pool correlates with films Nicolas Cage appeared in
- Divorce rate in Maine correlates with per capita consumption of margarine
- People who drowned after falling out of a fishing boat correlates with the marriage rate in Kentucky. (Ok, this correlation may not be so spurious).

Don't Step in The Name Droppings

When I began my career in advertising, the rule of thumb was to try to work for the biggest agency on the biggest client possible. Why? Because bigger clients typically had bigger budgets. Bigger budgets meant you had the resources to do "cooler" things. My big-agency buddies were exposed to exciting projects like negotiating professional sports sponsorships and Times Square signage deals. They were creating national advertising campaigns and rubbing elbows with celebrities on the Forbes yacht.

I began my career working for smaller regional ad agencies. It was good work for good clients with good people, but we were admittedly lower on the industry hierarchy compared to the big boys. We didn't have large budgets. As a result, we had to be scrappy and creative and frugal in order to help our clients meet their objectives. It wasn't as glamorous as working for one of the bigger shops, but it was challenging and fun. One key advantage to working for a smaller agency was working directly with the more experienced, higher-level executives. That was something my big-agency friends didn't have. It was the perfect learning environment for a young man just getting started.

One Monday morning, the entire agency (maybe 35 employees) crammed into our large conference room for the weekly traffic meeting. We were introduced to a new employee who had come to us from the global advertising agency, J. Walter Thompson. We weren't given her full story, but because she had worked at J. Walter, she had immediate credibility with everyone in the room. She was maybe a year or two older than I.

A few weeks into her tenure, I picked up on a little quirk of this seemingly accomplished young woman. At least once in every meeting she would begin a sentence with "When I was at J. Walter..." And the room would go silent to listen to whatever she had to say. It reminded me of the classic E.F. Hutton advertising line, "When E.F. Hutton talks, people listen." Generally, what she had to say after her E.F. Hutton intro was not particularly impressive, but no one else seemed to notice. They were mesmerized by the big-agency reference. She constantly used that tactic to command attention and it worked every time. When J. Walter talked, people listened.

Once I picked up on her little trick, it drove me crazy; it took me a little while to understand why it bothered me so much. She was leveraging the good name of her previous employer to establish her own credibility when, in fact, working at a big-name agency is no guarantee of competence. Her name dropping was a form of *illusory correlation*, which is the belief that there is a relationship between two variables when little or no relationship actually exists. As another mental shortcut that helps us avoid the paralysis of analyzing every situation, it is both a blessing and a curse. We all do it. It helps us get through the day, but it also prevents us from keeping a truly open mind.

I vowed never to establish my own credibility by name dropping. It was a matter of honor.

Over a decade later, I found myself working for Victoria's Secret. By that time, I was the one with a resume full of big brand names that others admired, but this was my first stop in the fashion retail industry. That's why they hired me, in fact: to bring a fresh perspective to the PINK brand and create their first brand-growth plan.

In the beginning of my tenure there, I was occasionally reminded that I had no experience in fashion retail, therefore, my opinion would be taken with a grain of salt. As the business growth strategist, I took a deep dive into the business, ramped up my knowledge of the industry, and fairly quickly had sound ideas to contribute.

Then it happened. One day, we were in a planning meeting with the leaders of the brand. I attempted to add my two cents to the conversation, but was rudely shut down by one of the members of the leadership team. In essence I was asked, "What do you know about retail?" Before I knew what was coming out of my mouth I heard, "When I was at Coke...." Oh no! Did I just say that? I did. And the room went silent and listened to my idea.

I had broken my vow. I had dropped a name. The worst part? It worked. I felt ashamed, but I did get my point across in that meeting. In time, I built enough genuine credibility with the PINK team that they no longer questioned my understanding of fashion retail. I also renewed my vow never to name drop again.

My ideas at Victoria's Secret were no better because I had previously worked for The Coca-Cola Company, but that association helped my credibility. Similarly, the young lady from J. Walter Thompson wasn't necessarily any more competent or talented than anyone else working at our "mid-sized" agency because she had previously worked for the bigger brand name agency. In fact, we didn't know what she actually accomplished or learned there.

Years later, I'm often introduced as the guy who managed the brand-growth plan for Victoria's Secret PINK. It gives me instant credibility and people find it fascinating. But I promise I won't drop that name... unless I really need to.

The Asian (Dis)Advantage

Heidi was a young business owner. She was petite in stature, with dark brown hair in a neat bun and stylish glasses. She spoke with a distinct accent; she was one of the many immigrants who had come to the United States in search of a better life.

We were talking one day and, completely out of the blue, she stated that she wasn't Mexican, she was from Guatemala. It was an answer to a question I had not asked; it was so out of context, I wasn't sure what to say. My response was to nod my head in acknowledgement, say "Oh, ok," and change the subject.

But her comment stuck with me. Why did she feel compelled to tell me her country of origin? She obviously thought it mattered or she wouldn't have brought up the topic unprompted. Maybe she had encountered the question before and wanted to answer it and move on. She also must have believed that Guatemala had a greater status in my eyes than Mexico; otherwise, why would she compare the two countries?

It turned out that Heidi was addressing a common stereotype based on place of origin, one that assigns less-desirable characteristics to people from one country and more-desirable characteristics to people from other countries. Obviously, and unfortunately, Heidi had experienced the effects of this prejudice many times and sought to avoid the consequences of being negatively stereotyped.

One of the more dangerous examples of false cause is stereotyping based on ethnicity or place of origin. This is an example of *in-group bias*, automatically favoring your own group over people viewed as outside your group. We make assumptions about belief systems, character traits, and behavior based on group affiliation. Our self-esteem is wrapped up in groups with which we associate. If our group is considered superior, we consider ourselves superior by association. This bias, and the behavior that accompanies it, are displayed everywhere divisions are possible: geography, politics, wealth, religion, and race.

After Europeans settled in North America, they were leery of newcomers. They believed that strangers were usually there for nefarious reasons or at the very least would compete for resources. The established settlers felt threatened by each new wave of immigrants: Irish, Mexicans, Chinese, Polish, Russians, Japanese, Italians, Cubans, Puerto Ricans, and Germans. This attitude was ironic: for a period of history, the most dangerous immigrants were the Europeans themselves.

Europeans marginalized and displaced indigenous populations to the point that, today, Native Americans make up only 1.7% of the population in the United States. Another group victimized by this protectionist belief system were those of African descent. Given the history of slavery in this country, African Americans are without question the flag-bearers of the destructive nature of stereotypes and discrimination. There have been volumes written about the history of racism in this country; I cannot do it justice with one chapter of this book.

Many Americans are unaware of this, but Asian immigrants also faced systematic discrimination in the United States. Both local and federal legislation prohibited them from competing with groups who immigrated to America earlier, mostly those of European descent.

The first major wave of Asian immigration came from China, during the gold rush in the mid-1800's. The early miners were met with discrimination in the form of legislation like the Foreign Miner Tax, which was only levied on Chinese miners. They also worked as merchants, gardeners, laundry workers, and domestic help, and were seen as an economic threat to Californians because of job competition. The Chinese Exclusion Act of 1882 blocked additional immigration from China and prevented Chinese immigrants from becoming citizens of the United States. They were also forbidden to own real estate, get an education, marry whites, or live in certain areas of the city. In order to survive, they formed their own isolated communities, which were the first Chinatowns.

Later groups emigrating from Asia were met with similar discrimination and hardship. One of the more egregious acts of discrimination against Asians came in 1942 during WWII, when President Roosevelt issued Executive Order 9066, imprisoning over 100,000 people of Japanese ancestry until the order was rescinded in 1945. Two-thirds of those detained were American citizens. The economic, social, and psychological cost was beyond measure.

Now, imagine reading about a group that is the smallest of the four major ethnicities in their country, has been systematically discriminated against, prevented from assimilating, and forced into isolated communities. You might assume that group would reside at the bottom of the social pyramid, wouldn't you?

Not by a long shot. Today, people of Asian descent are most commonly stereotyped as hard working, intelligent, successful, and serious about education. The question is, how did this small minority overcome the many obstacles of prejudice to be associated with such positive stereotypes?

One common theory supporting these stereotypes is that Asians, as a group, are more intelligent than other ethnic groups. There is little evidence to back that up. Even if Asians as a group had a slight intelligence advantage, the fact is, having the capability or threshold to achieve something doesn't guarantee that one will actually achieve it. For example, most people who excel at basketball are tall, but not all tall people excel at basketball.

The theory I support for the evolution of these stereotypes is that the Asian-American *culture* emphasizes educational achievement, which drives families to commit resources to childhood development in a far greater way than other ethnic groups. This investment in resources provides their children with a leg up in our education system. Acceptance into a prestigious college or university is seen as a return on an investment after years of hard work and sacrifice.

By all accounts the Asian advantage appears to be effort. The Asian *dis*advantage is society's reaction to that success: rather than celebrating it, we still feel threatened, and put up barriers to protect or redirect resources.

In his article *For Asian Americans, A Changing Landscape on College Admissions*, Los Angeles Times writer, Frank Shyong, reported on a Princeton University study that attempted to determine how ethnicity affects admissions, using the benchmark of SAT scores. The study hypothesized that some applicants were given "bonus" points on their SAT scores to provide an advantage to students of underrepresented ethnicities on college campuses. Mathematically, it appeared as if African Americans were given 230 bonus points and Hispanics were awarded 185 bonus points. Meanwhile, 50 points were *deducted* from the scores of Asian Americans.

Why would college admissions personnel systematically penalize Asian students? According to Shyong, it's because Asian Americans represented a higher percentage of the student body than their share of the population of the United States. Many people in the Asian community believe college campuses are discriminating against applicants who identify as Asian solely because of their academic success.

In November 2014, an alliance of Asian-American groups filed a lawsuit against Harvard, citing discrimination against Asian applicants. They also filed complaints with the U.S. Justice Department's Civil Rights Division and the U.S. Education Department's Office for Civil Rights. If the Princeton study's theory is true, the United States is once again engaged in the systematic discrimination of a major ethnic minority group simply based on race or heritage.

What's interesting about this situation is that *effort* has nothing to do with the physical characteristics or genetic makeup of the many groups included in the census category known as Asians. There is a correlation between academic success and Asians as a group, but the cause of that success is falsely attributed to their ethnicity. A strong work ethic is fair game for imitation.

Atari's Pitfall

We assign good and bad traits to brands of all kinds: packaged goods, automobile manufacturers, retailers, universities, political parties, religions, etc. These *associations* influence how we feel about the people or things connected with those brands. For example, I mentioned to my friend Ed how much I liked a new car model from a certain German manufacturer and his response was, "(Those) drivers are jerks." The company makes a slew of models and styles of cars, SUVs, and motorcycles; for some reason Ed correlated *all* owners of this brand with a personality type (it wasn't Mercedes, by the way). Ed is an intelligent, successful, well-educated man, but to him the association was simple: ownership of this brand made a person a jerk.

Just how powerful are these associations? Remember, Pavlov's dogs salivated when they heard bells ringing, even though ringing bells and food have no true relationship. Pavlov created an association that affected the dogs' physiology to the point where a ringing bell triggered the physical response of salivation. The relationships we perceive between two people or objects can be either positive or negative. In the example above, Ed was trying to influence me not to buy a certain brand of automobile, so he created a negative association with that brand and its owners. Associations are very powerful and often work on an unconscious level.

What if you were a talented video game programmer who had developed some of the most popular games of your time, selling millions of units? What if you had been handpicked by Steven Spielberg to develop a video game based on his latest blockbuster movie? What if you created that game in a record time of less than six weeks, sold over one million copies, and were then blamed for the crash of the entire video game industry? That's exactly what happened to a promising young developer named Howard Scott Warshaw.

In the late 1970's, our culture was fascinated with space and technology. On the small screen, we watched programs like Space 1999, Battlestar Galactica, Buck Rogers in the 25th Century, and old Star Trek reruns. The blockbuster movies of the time included Star Wars, Star Wars: The Empire Strikes Back, Star Wars: Return of the Jedi, Star Trek: The Motion Picture, Alien, Close Encounters of the Third Kind, and Steven Spielberg's E.T. the Extra-Terrestrial. Science fiction entertainment filled our imaginations with the possibilities of space exploration and the use of futuristic technology.

About that same time a company named Atari introduced its 2600 video game console for home use. For those of a certain age, the Atari 2600 was our introduction to computers. We were able to bring the arcade games we loved into our living rooms and play as many games as our parents would purchase. No quarters necessary!

By 1982, almost every kid I knew owned an Atari console. In fact, by 1983 there were about 10 million Atari 2600s in the market. The early games, like Pong (1977), are laughably basic compared to today's technology; at the time, it was truly amazing. The graphics and technology continued to improve with games like Space Invaders (1980), Asteroids (1981), Ms. Pac-Man (1982), Pitfall! (1982), and Frogger (1982).

When Spielberg's E.T. was released in theaters in June 1982, it quickly became the blockbuster hit of the summer and held the position of highest-grossing film of all time for a decade. Based on the immense popularity of the film, Atari purchased the rights to develop an E.T. video game. Steven Spielberg immediately called Howard Scott Warshaw.

Warshaw, just in his mid-twenties, had already developed Atari's bestselling original title to date, *Yars' Revenge*, as well as a video game based on Spielberg's *Raiders of the Lost Ark*. The director and programmer had hit it off, so Spielberg chose Warshaw for the development of the E.T. game.

Warshaw accepted the challenge, even though he would only have six weeks to complete the entire project. This was a ridiculously short timeframe to develop a new video game, but it had to be ready for the upcoming holiday retail sales season. Warshaw worked around the clock to meet the tight timeline. Completing the project on time was nothing less than extraordinary. Spielberg himself approved the final version, but there wasn't time to test the concept with consumers. With the popularity of the movie and a proven winner designing the video game, Atari took a gamble by manufacturing around four million cartridges of the E.T. game.

The game became one of the top-ten bestselling Atari 2600 video games, with an estimated 1.5 million copies sold. Unfortunately for Atari—and Warshaw—it soon faced critical backlash. Both critics and gamers expressed a strong dislike for the game. The E.T. video game would come to be known as one of the worst games of all time. Two and a half million copies were either unsold or returned. Even with the high number of units sold, the game was considered a failure.

On the heels of the E.T. video game debacle, both Atari and the gaming industry crashed. In 1983, Atari's CEO, Ray Kassar, was forced out; over the next few years, parts of the company were sold off to other players in the market. The industry would take years to recover. Simply because of the very public disappointment of E.T., and its correlation in time with the crash, Warshaw was blamed for bringing down not just his company but the entire gaming industry.

Because of the false cause of association, Warshaw's career as a programmer was over. He would go on to write books, produce documentaries, and eventually become a licensed psychotherapist in Silicon Valley. His experiences as a programmer gave him a unique ability to help people in the hi-tech community.

Was Warshaw to blame for the downfall of Atari and the video game industry? While he became the poster child for the collapse, he did not cause it. The market's response to E.T. certainly didn't help the situation, but a number of other factors contributed to the Atari and video game industry crash of 1983:

Saturation: According to the US census, in 1983 there were around 60 million kids between 10–24 years old. Video game enthusiasts skew male, so the buying market came largely from the 30 million male children. As we mentioned earlier, approximately 10 million Atari 2600 consoles were in use at that time. That means one out of every three males between the ages of 10 and 24 had an Atari 2600 in the home. A significant number of the other two males in that equation were not part of the buying market: not every kid liked video games, not every parent wanted their kids to play video games, and not every household could afford a console. Given those points, the buying market was saturated.

Competition: Atari's direct competitors were other game console brands like Odyssey 2 by Magnavox (1978), Intellivision by Mattel (1980), and ColecoVision (1982). Atari also faced competition on two other fronts: third-party developers and the growing popularity of the personal computer, or PC. In 1979, a group of former Atari programmers began developing and distributing game cartridges under the name Activision. They were the first third-party developers for video game consoles. Before Activision, each manufacturer made cartridges that worked only on their consoles. In the next few years, other game developers would enter the market, further diluting Atari's share.

By 1982, PC sales were really taking off. Third-party developers took advantage of the opportunity by designing game software to play on PCs. Adding games to all the other functionality of early PCs made them a worthwhile investment, shifting consumer dollars away from Atari and the game console industry as a whole.

Poor inventory planning: E.T. wasn't the only failure for Atari in 1982; Pac-Man also fell well short of sales expectations. Like E.T., Pac-Man was rushed to market and faced its share of criticism. The real problem wasn't the game—Atari sold around seven million cartridges—it was overproduction. They produced approximately 12 million cartridges, more than the number of consoles in the market. It doesn't take an MBA or mathematician to realize Atari had been overly optimistic in their production planning and sales estimates.

The economy: About the time Atari was manufacturing 16 million E.T. and Pac-Man game cartridges, the U.S. was at the peak of a recession. In fact, according the U.S. Bureau of Labor Statistics, in December 1983, the nationwide unemployment rate was 10.8%, the highest since the Great Depression of 1929. Many people didn't have the disposable income to buy a gaming console or game cartridges. Those who did were reluctant to spend their disposable income on a game.

The evidence is overwhelming. The crash occurred shortly after he took a calculated risk that failed, but Howard Scott Warshaw was not to blame for the failure of Atari and he did not cause the video game industry to collapse in 1983. He was the fall guy, caught in the causation/correlation trap.

Why Men Are Smarter Than Women

It's true. Meta-analyses from studies done around the world confirm that, on average, men are more intelligent than women... by a whopping 3–5 IQ points. You have probably already guessed that while this data is technically true, it is misleading. The genetic correlation with intelligence isn't with gender. It's with height.

For every additional inch in height, the average IQ increases by around 0.4 points. On average, men are taller than women. That height advantage could lead us to believe that men are (ever so slightly) smarter than women. On the other hand, women are smarter than men of the same height. That means on a comparable basis, adjusted for height, women are (also ever so slightly) smarter than men. What was it that Mark Twain said about lies, damn lies, and statistics?

There is a correlation between height and intelligence, but don't hit the panic button if you are "vertically challenged." Intelligence is about potential, not certainties. People with high IQs have the ability to comprehend complicated concepts faster than people with comparably lower IQs, but as we learned in the *Asian (Dis)Advantage*, that is only one factor of many that determine success.

Despite a relatively equal playing field in terms of intelligence, tall men do enjoy a definite social advantage. In fact, our society is pretty open about our prejudice and discrimination against short men. There are many factors at play to explain our general preference for taller men, both at work and in relationships.

Height has traditionally been an indicator of health, wealth, and status. As Harvard professor Dr.

Nancy Etcoff suggests, inherited genes provide us with only the possibility to grow tall. Height is determined by the acquisition of resources and exposure to conditions enabling growth; the greatest determinant is better nutrition. This explains why upper classes have historically been taller than lower classes, and wealthier nations tend to have taller populations than poorer nations. Better nutrition and healthcare enable populations to realize their potential height. By contrast, having a smaller stature is associated with a lack of resources.

We choose leaders who fit our stereotypical image of a leader, and we always choose a leader. Any time two or more people gather, a natural social dynamic of mammals is to automatically and unconsciously establish a hierarchy of dominance. As in the animal kingdom, the dominant one tends to be the largest. (By the way, do you know how to determine the socially dominant person in a group? He or she is the person that no one talks over when they speak.)

It should come as no surprise, then, that the U.S. presidency has been won by the taller of the major party candidates in nearly 90% of the elections since 1900. The winning candidate is generally also taller than the average citizen. The average 20th century US president is 6' 0'' tall; the average US male is 5' 9.3" tall, nearly three inches shorter.

Tall men display leadership qualities because their physical stature provides a sense of security and protection that inspires us to follow. Studies show tall men tend to have higher self-esteem; they are also happier, more confident, and less likely to be jealous of others. Given the social advantages of being tall, these characteristics are hardly surprising: the privileged rarely have cause for jealousy.

But social advantages may come with a cost. Dr. Susan Heitler calls a pattern of male narcissism exhibited in taller men *Tall Man Syndrome*. She wrote, "Narcissism is a potential price of success when you are taller than, more famous than, smarter than, more athletic than (others).... (A "standout" child) doesn't have to concern himself with the feelings or concerns of other kids."

Short men, on the other hand, face systemic discrimination from a young age. As boys on the playground, they struggle to establish a place in the social hierarchy, often facing or fleeing from bullies in physical confrontations. As teenagers, they must overcome ego-threatening height biases to break into the dating scene. As adults, they are passed over for taller counterparts, though they may be every bit as qualified.

In her studies of work competence based on height, Dr. Etcoff confirms that there "were no differences in the quality or quantity of work performed based on height." One doesn't need to be tall to be an effective doctor, lawyer, programmer, or business leader. Yet, height is still a factor in career success. If you want to be a U.S. president or CEO, height helps.

Have you ever described someone as having a *Napoleon complex*? I have. A complex is a psychological term for any protective reflex to avoid the emotional pain of a traumatic experience, usually from childhood. Anything associated with that trauma triggers a flood of emotional and behavioral events, often unconsciously. Therefore, someone with a complex may have a distorted view of a current situation due to an irrational and emotional response to a traumatic trigger.

To be honest, I didn't make the connection that using the term Napoleon complex is based my personal height bias until I began researching this book. But think about it: when tall men are aggressive, we call them assertive, powerful, in control. When short men exhibit aggressive behavior to overcome a societal bias or discrimination, we say they have a psychological imbalance.

Our biases and behavior have a very real impact on the lives of others. The next time you label someone with the Napoleon complex (or any other complex for that matter), think of what they have had to endure to develop those feelings of inferiority. Perhaps his or her behavior is in response to how they have been treated. Or maybe our perception of their behavior is based on biases and fallacies tucked away in our unconscious minds. It's a complex issue.

The Problem with Pedigree

The perception of elite universities, such as Ivy League institutions, is that they provide a golden ticket to career success for their graduates. In fact, there actually is a correlation between attending a top university and having a successful career. In 2013, thirty women on the Forbes 100 Most Powerful Women list attended an Ivy League college. They make more money, too. A PayScale.com study revealed that the return on investment at elite institutions is at least 80% higher than other schools. The estimated 30-year return on investment of an Ivy League education is around $1.2 million. So yes, on average, graduates of prestigious colleges enjoy greater levels of success when the success metric is compensation.

The question is this: does the school make the student or does the student make the school? While there is a positive correlation between graduates of elite colleges and higher incomes, the schools themselves do not "cause" alumni success. It is no secret that prestigious schools are highly selective. They choose the best students and the best students tend to achieve more in life. However, an enlightening 30-year study by Alan Krueger and Stacy Dale shows the key indicator to future success is actually SAT score, not the institution of higher learning. They found that students who were accepted by prestigious schools, but instead chose to attend less-selective colleges earned salaries on par with Ivy League graduates. Even students who were rejected from elite schools, but had similarly high SAT scores as elite school graduates, earned comparable salaries to Ivy Leaguers. It's the quality of the student that drives success, not the brand name of the university. Elite schools aren't necessarily better at educating; they're better at attracting really smart, driven students.

Another misconception about graduates of elite colleges is that they were among the most qualified applicants. Not all students are admitted due to merit alone. Some spots are taken by less-qualified candidates due to family connections. In her article, *Harvard, Stanford Reject 95 Percent of Applicants This Year*, Janet Lorin reported that "A quarter of admissions officers [among the 400 officers polled] said they felt pressured to admit less-qualified applicants because they had business, political and other connections to the school, and 16% said they gave preference to children or siblings of alumni."

Graduating from an elite university is a wonderful achievement and provides noteworthy advantages. In addition to the boost of having a prestigious brand name on one's resume, these institutions connect alumni with a network of influential people. That said, having a degree from a prestigious university doesn't ensure greater success than someone with like talent from a less-selective school. In other words, attending a less-selective school isn't a career death sentence. While there are correlations between standardized test scores and academic achievement, your success in life depends on your talent, your work ethic, your skill set, and, ultimately, your decisions. Choose wisely.

On the Flip Side of False Cause

On the flip side, if we accept that we human beings look for causation and correlation to explain events and behavior, we can use that knowledge to our advantage. Here are a few ideas to use the false-cause fallacy to influence the decision making of others:

Create a positive (or negative) association. Businesses employ celebrities to endorse their products or services because of the principle of association. You can use this same technique to persuade people to your way of thinking. Connect what you are selling (product, service, idea, candidate, etc.) to something or someone who embodies the characteristics that support your value proposition. It could be a celebrity, a powerful internal sponsor from your organization, or perhaps even your competition.

I spent the first half of my advertising career trying to convince clients that a clean, uncluttered design aesthetic is more effective than a busy "circus" ad design. My advice was usually met with resistance as clients wanted to include every piece of mundane information about their product or service in every communication or advertisement. Too much information is overwhelming and typically ignored.

Then came Apple, Inc. Their simple, clean design aesthetic has become synonymous with their brand. It looks tasteful and sophisticated. Now, clients ask for a clean design like that of Apple. So, when I want a client to use a more uncluttered design, I'll simply reference the Apple's design look, "Don't you want a clean, sophisticated look... like Apple's?" Argument over. Thank you, Apple!

Name drop. This is another way to use the power of association. As much as I dislike name dropping, when we need to influence others, affiliating ourselves with someone or something credible is an effective tactic. That affiliation can be a school ("at Harvard we learned to..."), a place of employment ("at J. Walter we approached it this way..."), or a credible person ("When I worked with Thomas Edison, he always said...").

Provide a lucky rabbit's foot. Belief may be the most powerful concept in decision making and influence. When fear is holding someone back from making the right decision or performing a task, take advantage of the placebo effect and give him or her a "lucky" talisman or rabbit's foot. It can often boost belief and confidence when needed to perform a task under pressure. Examples include a lucky pen, tie, or brief case, or perhaps a lucky bat, ball, or hat. The object or talisman could be anything, really, but it should be relevant to the situation.

Beware of the self-fulfilling prophecy. Verbalizing self-doubt is a big red flag. Sometimes a person uttering self-deprecating remarks is trying to gain your favor, or fishing for a compliment to boost self-confidence. Other times, they might be revealing a self-defeating *internal dialogue,* the conversation they have with themselves under times of stress, which can lead to a *self-fulfilling prophecy.* This is a fear-based thought pattern that takes place when a negative belief (false or otherwise) evokes behavior leading to the realization of the negative belief.

When someone believes they cannot accomplish something, they will often unconsciously find ways to fail. Therefore, when he or she shares a lack of confidence or conviction in their abilities to deliver on an important task, take action to prevent their failure. Help them to successfully complete the task any way you can. If they fail, their prophecy would be validated and their confidence in achieving similar tasks could be compromised.

We never saw it coming. Failure is a part of life and some people deal with it better than others. As we learned earlier, when someone fails they might exhibit a greater sensitivity to defeat. To keep someone from giving up, try using the "we never saw it coming" justification. Pump up his or her confidence by using false cause to attribute the failure to external factors, while giving them credit for any wins or gains. This technique leverages the *self-serving attribution bias*, the belief that positive outcomes are within our control, while negative outcomes are outside our control. "Thanks to you, we won" or "it's someone/something else's fault we lost." This approach is simply an ego-saving device that might prove helpful in getting a person dealing with failure to get back on the horse.

We don't always get what we deserve. Howard Scott Warshaw didn't deserve to get blackballed from the world of programming; students of Asian heritage don't deserve the challenge of higher entrance requirements; and short men don't deserve workplace discrimination. The world is inherently unfair and we do not always get what we deserve.

Sometimes that's a good thing. Another instance of the false-cause fallacy is the *just-world phenomenon*, the belief that the world is fair and people generally get what they deserve. This explains why victims are sometimes blamed for crimes against them. The just-world phenomenon is a dangerous thought pattern that has been used to justify witch hunts, slavery, genocide, and other acts for which there can be no justification.

Unfortunately, people with this belief system will not always listen to reason. Therefore, the most effective weapon to fight a dangerous justification from a just-world thinker is to discredit their justification with a negative association. "Evil" historical character references are common. (You know the usual suspects; I won't list them here.) While you probably won't change the just-world thinker's mind, you will tarnish their credibility in the eyes of their audience.

Beware of the victim mentality: Success is the best revenge. We have all been the victim of an offense—some serious and others minor. On the positive side, victimhood protects our self-concept by pointing the blame for negative conditions away from us. On the negative side, unwarranted blame and victimhood can divest us of the responsibility to own our wellbeing. The habitual practice of blame leads to feelings of indignation, resentment, and discontent. Even when your feelings are justified, the victim mentality won't lead you to success and happiness.

When a decision maker takes on the victim mentality, it can negatively impact their will to move forward. They can get stuck. Remind them that success is the best revenge. We are all the master of our own self-concept, if not our circumstances. The choices we make should reinforce our goals for happiness and personal wellbeing.

●●●●●

MOMENTARY LAPSE OF REASON:
Too Much Information

Mary was overwhelmed. She enjoyed designing jewelry as a hobby. Pieces were sold or given to friends from makeshift displays in her home. The response to her jewelry was so enthusiastic she decided to make it a small business. As any start-up founder would tell you, launching a new business is exceedingly difficult. As Mary soon learned, business owners, especially new ones, make countless decisions every day about design, pricing, sourcing, marketing, distribution, accounting, and on and on. Every time she made one decision, three more issues popped up requiring her attention.

Mary's vocation was physical therapy. She was also a mother of three, a wife, a daughter, a sister, and a friend. Her formal training wasn't in business, so she relied on experienced friends and family for advice. She often received conflicting points of view on the same topic; the deluge of information only made her decisions more difficult to make.

Too much information can be just as big a barrier to decision making as too little information. Unable to discern which data is essential to make an informed choice, we fall into analysis paralysis.

Our minds become overloaded with useless information, and that cognitive overload triggers autopilot thinking.

It is vital to remember that not all information is necessary to make a sound choice. Typically, just one or two factors carry most of the weight in our decision. Find them and filter everything else out.

This was precisely the advice I gave Mary. Her first task was to write down the choices available to her. Then she was to determine the single most important piece of data, or decision factor, to her. Finally, she was to make a decision and move on. This process was much more palatable for her than analyzing countless points of useless information. And if her decision turned out to be wrong? Well, then she would simply take stock of the new situation and make an adjustment.

In most situations, we have the ability to decide, read, and react. Make your decision, then read the results. If it becomes apparent that a decision is not working, react by making a change. In the real world, variables change all the time. Even with perfect information the right choice might become the wrong choice if and when environmental factors evolve.

When you find yourself faced with too much information, take stock of your top priorities. Then pick the key factor, decide, read, and react.

THE FOURTH DEADLY SIN

FAMILARITY: Being Overly Attracted
to the Familiar

The Right Mix

Mixing a drink can be as simple as combining one part whiskey with two parts cola on ice, or as difficult as "muddling" an authentic Mojito. Muddling is the process of gently releasing the concentrated essential oils from mint leaves without tearing the mint into little pieces. It's a difficult and time-consuming process; a hurried or inexperienced bartender will hand you a glass full of soggy leaves. No one wants that. What a wonderful opportunity for a pre-made bar mixer!

Years ago, I managed a portfolio of bar mixer products for a large beverage company. A bar mixer is any beverage—including soft drinks, flavored syrups, juices, and fruit purees—blended with distilled spirits to make a "mixed drink." High-end bars and restaurants will typically make their own mixers using fresh ingredients, but the process is time consuming and the ingredients are expensive. As a result, most bars choose ready-made mixers. My portfolio featured well-known brands, vast distribution, and high-quality products at a slightly premium price. Good stuff.

The most promising category in the portfolio was our non-alcoholic frozen mixer line. We had licensed the name of our frozen mixers from a popular spirits brand, which gave the product instant credibility with our customers. In addition to mixed drinks, these frozen purees made delicious specialty drinks, smoothies, and shakes. It was a relatively new line compared to our other products, and our market share was still rather low.

One day, an internal representative from one of our major fast-food customer account teams approached me about the idea of offering our fruit-flavored mixers to their customer. They were looking for a tasty, easy to use puree for a new smoothie line they were developing. If this company decided to use our purees, my portfolio sales would explode. Their biggest complaint, of course, was the name. The fast food giant was leery of making smoothies for kids using a brand name connected with alcohol.

The opportunity to rebrand the frozen puree products for fast-food restaurants was intoxicating (pun intended). I developed new packaging for this market and used the name of a popular fruit juice brand our company owned, which also had instant recognition and credibility. There would be no changes to the puree, just new packaging. My thinking at the time was that existing customers would get the same great product and our new customers could avoid the association with alcohol. What could go wrong?

We were so excited about entering the fast-food market that we expedited the production of the new packaging and merchandising. I personally visited the food processing plant where the puree was to be poured into our new containers and observed the very first case of the smoothie line come through.

The packaging came in large sheets of printed cardboard material. These sheets rolled through an automated assembly line, which folded them into the shape of a large milk carton. The machinery didn't miss a beat. Our mixer product was poured into a carton with our original mixer brand and the very next instant it was poured into a container labeled with our new fruit smoothie logo. Just like that. Same product, new package. It took all of a second to make the change.

To launch the "new" brand, the President of our division sent a letter to every existing customer explaining the change and assuring them that they could expect the same delicious product in the new packaging. I went on a road show promoting the name change. I conducted training seminars at each regional office around the country. Collateral materials were provided and samples were delivered for the sales staff to share with both new and existing customers. All bases were covered. Or, so I thought.

The very first week of the smoothie introduction, I received a call from a sales representative on the west coast. One of our biggest customers was not happy with the new product. I asked our sales rep to sit in on a conference call on the customer's side and to bring both "old" and "new" puree products to the meeting. We would have a little taste test while on the call. They were exactly the same product from the exact same batch. This should be easy to fix.

Four or five people, including my sales rep, compared several flavors of each product. The client declared the new smoothie product inferior in taste to the former mixer product. He was clearly agitated and said this new product would negatively impact his sales. How dare we change the product formula!

I explained the rationale and process and assured him the products were exactly the same, from the same batch of puree, in fact. The only difference in the product he sampled was the name on the carton.

He didn't believe me. In fact, he implied that I was lying.

My customer had fallen for the "sin" of familiarity. Familiarity is another shortcut our brains use when on autopilot. It takes the analysis out of decision making when we simply choose the familiar. In most instances, this shortcut provides a time saving advantage; however, it is a gateway to complacency. Familiarity lulls us into making poor decisions because the familiar choice isn't always the best choice.

A client of mine, we'll call him Jim, shared the frustration of losing a new business pitch to a less-qualified competitor. In fact, he said his bid was better in every way compared to the winner: price, speed, capabilities, you name it. Unfortunately, the situation was common for his company: they had invested very little to build their brand recognition, so most customers had never heard of them. Familiarity is a prerequisite of trust. In Jim's case, the business went to a more trusted brand name—a familiar name. A name the decision maker could justify to his boss and peers. It felt like the safe choice.

In my own case, to keep my unhappy customer's business, I decided to "cave." After thanking him for his honest feedback, I said I understood how important it was to maintain the integrity of the original formulas to ensure the quality of our customers' finished drink products. I apologized for any trouble this change had caused him and his business, and promised to use the original formulas in all our smoothies moving forward.

Everything I said was true. Misleading, but true. The product wouldn't change because it was the original formula. My customer was influenced by the *mere-exposure effect*, the psychological term for the sin of familiarity, is when we tend to prefer things with which we are familiar. Merely being exposed to something (product, candidate, idea, etc.) is enough to cause us to prefer it over something with which we are less familiar. And the more exposure we have to something, the more we tend to like it. He loved the original—familiar—product and I had changed it. Because we value consistency and are threatened by change, something as minor as replacing a logo on the package was enough to affect his perception of the product flavor.

My customer was also experiencing sensation transference, the unconscious transfer of our impressions of the package to the product inside. In essence, the product experience is a combination of the product and its package. Dr. Nancy Etcoff explains, "People like to believe that looks don't matter. But every marketing executive knows that packaging and image are as important as the product, if not more so. We treat appearances not just as a source of pleasure or shame but as a source of information."

I never heard another complaint from that disgruntled customer; he must have become a fan of our new smoothie... logo.

Buzzword Bingo

Buzzword Bingo (also called Bullshit Bingo) was a popular game played by the minions of corporate America. The game was simple: a "board" or paper with 25 squares (five columns by five rows) was filled with the most annoying buzzwords and phrases in popular use. When one of these words or phrases was used in a meeting, presentation, or speech, the bingo players would mark the box with the offending term. When five consecutive squares were filled vertically, horizontally, or diagonally, the winner was to discreetly signal, "BINGO!"

This game was developed in reaction to the near-constant use of what I call replacement terms. Replacement terms are new words and phrases used to replace perfectly good "old" words and phrases. The purpose of this behavior was to make old concepts sound new again, which was (and is) a standard business practice of most management consultants and newly minted MBA's. We love to reinvent the wheel!

Because I am both a consultant and an MBA, I unapologetically use replacement terms as often as

I can, secretly hoping to hear someone scream, "BINGO!"

Here are just a few examples of buzzwords that replaced existing terms in the conference rooms of corporate America at the time this story took place:

Actualize	Instead of...	Produce, realize, accomplish, or do
Synergy	Instead of...	Cooperation
Bucketize	Instead of...	Categorize
Touch base	Instead of...	Meet
Circle back	Instead of...	Return
Key Takeaways	Instead of...	Conclusions, impressions, or points
Action item	Instead of...	Task
Results driven	Instead of...	Employed

I'm sure you can "reimagine" a few of your own.

One day at lunch, I shared my Bingo results with a colleague (we'll call him Dave to protect the guilty) and we talked about how these words became popular in our corporate culture. I had recently read Malcolm Gladwell's wonderful book *The Tipping Point*. Dave and I decided to test the theories in the book by introducing a new buzzword into the lexicon of our corporation. How fast would it reach the tipping point of popularity?

We were both in marketing functions, but in different "silos" of the business. Our roles were similar enough, so we found a shared and often discussed aspect of our function to rename. The new buzzword was chosen from an episode of the comedy television show *Seinfeld*, one of our favorites. The word had to *sound* as if it could be used in the context of our marketing activity, even though it was not currently used to describe the activity. I will reveal neither the buzzword nor the renamed aspect of marketing because I would love for my former colleagues to guess.

Dave and I were rarely in meetings together, which meant we could cover more ground. It also made things a little intimidating because we didn't have an accomplice in the room for support. The plan was simple: whenever that marketing activity was discussed, we would call it our new buzzword. Our strategy was to use the term confidently and then quickly move the conversation along. An early challenge on the validity of the word would surely mean an early crash and burn for the experiment.

It didn't happen. No one challenged us. Ever. So, we kept using it and using it and using it. In fact, I never stopped. I still use the buzzword today. Maybe other marketers didn't challenge us because replacement words were often introduced into our corporate culture. Maybe the term just worked and people like using it. Who knows? Even seasoned marketers let it pass without batting an eye. That did not mean the experiment was a success... yet.

I noticed that my peers in other functions adopted the term first. They heard us, the experts, refer to something by our buzzword, so they just assumed we were using it correctly. We had no idea at the time, but we were leveraging two cognitive principles: *social proof* and the *mere-exposure effect.*

The principle of social proof was also at play in "The Dr. Fox Effect." As you will recall, we look to others to determine what is correct and will often modify our behavior based on the behavior of others. Dave and I provided our workmates with social proof by using the new buzzword in the context we had chosen. Dr. Alain Samson explains this phenomenon, "Sometimes we imitate others to fit in; other times we copy people we know because we're simply uncertain about the best choice. Our peers play an important part in this process."

Dave and I used the new term repeatedly and consistently. Our work teams were exposed to the buzzword often enough to become familiar with it. The proof came when other associates began using our term in meetings. But that wasn't the tipping point.

The tipping point came when a very senior-level executive used our buzzword in a "town hall meeting" presentation, addressing the hundreds and hundreds of people in our division. That's when other marketers began using the term. That was the social proof they needed.

Almost a decade later, my wife, also in marketing and familiar with our little social experiment, reported hearing our buzzword at her place of employment in the same context as we originally introduced it. Hypothesis proven. My sincerest apologies for adding a term to buzzword bingo.

Note: No marketers were injured in this social experiment.

The Incumbent Advantage

In 2014, prior to the election, the US congressional approval rating was just 11%, according to Politifact.com. With an overwhelming majority of the electorate disapproving of the performance of their elected officials, voters were sure to "throw the bums out of office." But did they? Not even close. In that election, 96.4% of incumbents were re-elected to office. That means less than 4% of the bums were thrown out of office. What happened? There was so much discontent with the electorate, one would think a wholesale change would take place, but it didn't.

Historically, the incumbent reelection rate is consistently high. In fact, the incumbent reelection rate in the House of Representatives has hit its lowest point of 85% only twice since the 1964 election. The Senate tends to be more volatile, but their lowest reelection rate in the past twenty years was 75% in 1986.

In 2010, a New York Times/CBS News poll showed that 80% of us believed congressional representatives were more likely to serve special interest groups than to faithfully represent their electorates. Despite our declared hatred of the institution, around 85% of incumbents were re-elected in 2010, and that was at the low end of the typical reelection rate. In 2012, the reelection rate climbed back up to about 90%. Reelection rates of incumbents have remained high regardless of public sentiment. Ironically, the position of congressman happens to be one of the most stable jobs in our country. As Senator Tom Coburn said, "in several election cycles in recent history, more incumbents died in office than lost reelection bids." Why do we keep reelecting a congress that we adamantly dislike?

Familiarity. Simply being in office leverages the benefits of familiarity. We associate the incumbent with the position they hold, whereas we do not view the challenger in in that role.

Also, while outspending a political opponent does not guarantee reelection, it sure helps to build awareness—and thus familiarity—with constituents. Incumbents tend to have greater "war chests" to spend on campaigning than their rivals do. While in office and wielding the power that comes with it, they hold fundraising events to stockpile funds for their next campaign. According to Paul Steinhauser and Robert Yoon of CNN, "On average, House incumbents outspent their rivals $1.7 million to $587,000, a ratio of almost a 3-1. Incumbent senators spent on average $10.7 million compared to $7.2 million for challengers."

It's not us, it's them. People hate congress, but they usually like their own representatives... at least a little more than the group as a whole. A 2013 Gallup poll revealed that while congressional approval was only 16% at the time, 46% of respondents approved of "the way the representative from your congressional district is handling his or her job." While that was not a high approval rate, it was much higher than the approval rate for all of congress. The fact is, it's easier to hate an institution than an actual person.

We hate to admit when we're wrong. If I previously voted for him, he's my guy. Voting for someone else would be admitting I made a mistake when I voted for him last time and our brains are wired to justify and defend our decisions.

We vote for the lesser of two evils. The real choices for candidates occur in the primary elections, but less than 16% of the electorate voted in the 2012 primaries. That leads us to the general elections where there are fewer choices—usually between a Republican, a Democrat, and a smaller party candidate thrown in for good measure. Roughly two-thirds of voters identify with either the Democrat or Republican parties. Even people who consider themselves Independents tend to favor one party over another. When in doubt, we vote for the candidate in the party with which we identify, even when we're not particularly fond of the candidate.

Why do we typically toe the party line? One reason is ignorance. Only one-third of U.S. citizens know the name of their House representative. Even fewer people know what he or she has done for the district. We identify ourselves based on a particular belief system and we vote for candidates that we feel share that belief system. Most voting districts predominantly support one party over the other; when an incumbent has the support of their party in a district, reelection is nearly automatic.

But the choice very often comes down to marketing. I found Todd Phillips piece *How Was 91 Percent of Congress Re-Elected Despite a 10 Percent Approval Rating?* quite provocative. He wrote: "Political parties are marketing organizations— brand names, teams complete with colors, and mascots that serve the needs of the ambitious politicians and the special interests that fund them." Do I identify with the red team or the blue team? Am I a donkey or an elephant? Do I identify with this ideology or that ideology?

Politicians take the techniques of sophisticated marketers to the extreme by vilifying the opposing ideology, using the principle of familiarity and whittling the voting decision down to a yes or no question. This little tactic of influence makes it easier for voters to identify the lesser of two evils: am I for this (person, position, issue, etc.) or against it? It is up to me and my vote to ensure that my ideology perseveres and the opposition fails.

Why Brands Make Us Feel Better

I have suffered from terrible allergies for most of my life. Through trial and error, my doctors and I have found a combination of medications that almost completely alleviate my symptoms. Some of my prescriptions are now available as generics. They offer the same active ingredient for much less than the original brand. My doctors encourage me to buy the generic forms of prescriptions when available, but do they work as well as the original branded medication?

In her article *The Truth About Generics VS Brand-Name Medications*, Beth Levine cited a study from the University of Cincinnati that investigated this topic. Researchers gave participants with Parkinson's disease two different "experimental" treatments. Subjects were told the medications were similar: the second medication should produce the same results as the first medication, but the first medication was more expensive.

The "expensive" medication produced a remark-able 28% improvement in patient motor skills compared to the "cheaper" medication. In reality, both medications were only saline solution and should not have produced any results.

If neither treatment in the Parkinson's experiment were actually medication, why would the more expensive treatment produce a better result than the cheaper treatment? Because we expect more expensive things to perform better, even when there is no evidence to support the belief. The positive outcomes experienced by the Parkinson's patients had to do with the *placebo effect,* not the supposed experimental medication itself.

Expectations matter. Product presentation—pricing, design aesthetic, packaging—affects customer experience and perception of value. These elements together form a brand, and brands create an expectation in the customer's mind. In essence, familiar brands engage our autopilot thinking. That is why generic medications mimic the packaging of the brands that they are replacing. The aesthetic of the packaging is associated with the expectation of a specific outcome, which is that of the branded medication. The generic is drafting off the familiarity of the branded product.

Familiarity is a powerful principle, which is why it is one of the seven deadly sins of decision making. Whether it is a candidate, an idea, a product, or a person, we gravitate to the familiar. When making important decisions, we need to remember that we tend to favor what we know—

often without even considering whether it is the best choice.

On the Flip Side of Familiarity

We are all biased toward things with which we are familiar, and this tendency affects our choices every day. It also affects the choices of others. Here are a few ways you might use familiarity to influence a decision maker:

Be the first to market (i.e., become the incumbent). There is truth to the phrase "timing is everything." Being first to market with anything (a new product, service, or idea) helps to solidify your place in the minds of consumers. Human beings desire stability and consistency. We like things to be familiar and predictable. This is why marketers so desperately want you to *try* their products. Once a decision is made, consumers will likely stick with that product for future purchases. Be the first to market and let your audience's mental autopilot do the rest.

Use slogans, tag lines, and catch phrases. Think of your influence strategy as a classic advertising campaign. If you are over the age of 40, I'll bet you can still remember the jingles from some of the iconic brands of your childhood... even though they have been out of use for decades. Remember the catchy little songs for BAND-AID, Oscar Mayer Hot

Dogs, Kit Kat, and Meow Mix? You don't need me to remind you of famous advertising slogans from Coca-Cola, Wheaties, M&Ms, or Maxwell House. Distill your message into a concise, easy to remember phrase—like a slogan. Keep it short, simple, and to the point. Daniel Kahneman, a psychologist and behavioral economist who was awarded the Nobel Memorial Prize in Economic Sciences, put it this way: "What you see is all there is.... We are convinced by advertising based on consistency and coherence, not the quality and quantity of information." What Kahneman meant was slogans, interesting tag lines, and catchy phrases get the audience's attention. Attention equals focus. And focus increases that thing's perceived importance in the audience's mind, and decreases the importance of other, often competing, options.

I would also add that the use of alliteration and rhyming to help your audience remember key phrases. That is why it is easier to remember songs and poems than a passage written in prose. Trial lawyers have been known to employ this method of influence as well. For example, in the O.J. Simpson trial in 1995, attorney Johnny Cochran famously and effectively planted this seed with the jury about a glove found at the crime scene: "If it doesn't fit, you must acquit." The prosecution had asked Simpson earlier in the trial to try on the glove. After a year in an evidence bag, and with

Simpson strategically avoiding his arthritis medication, the leather glove did not fit his hand. In a long, drawn-out, complicated trial, Cochran had given the jury a simple yes or no question to answer in the deliberation room. Regardless of how people felt about the outcome of the trial, this brilliant influence technique worked on the jury.

Politicians have long understood the power of an effective sound bite: "I like Ike"; "Are you better off than you were four years ago?"; "It's the economy, stupid." These messages are short, specific, and to the heart of the matter. Get your audience to focus on one issue and provide them with an obvious yes or no question. The answer leads them to your desired choice or behavior.

Repeat yourself again and again. We tend to believe statements that we have heard before more than things we hear for the first time. This is called the *illusion-of-truth effect.* When Dave and I introduced our buzzword into the lexicon of our corporate employer, we used it consistently over a long period of time. The time aspect of this equation is known as the *spacing effect,* also called the *lag effect.* We recall information better when we hear it repeated over a long period of time. The key here is patience. Consistency + time = results.

Plant the seed. When I worked in corporate America, if I needed to introduce an idea for approval, I would first "plant the seed" of the idea with as many individuals as I could through casual, one-on-one conversations. Then, in the formal meeting, I would prime the group by saying something like, "as many of you already know." This phrase does two things. First, it establishes familiarity with the idea. Second, it requires affirmation: they really did already know, because I had told them. Affirmation typically promotes a response in the form of a verbal agreement or head nod. If their heads were nodding, they became co-conspirators in the sale of the idea. When other members of the group saw their peers acknowledge the idea, it was usually enough social proof to seal the deal.

(Re)Write history. Our memories are not as factually accurate as we might think. In fact, our memories include a myriad of inaccuracies because we inadvertently fill in the gaps with our beliefs, desires, and expectations. We unconsciously make things up. Unfortunately, we believe these memories to be factual accounts.

Our memories are prone to something called *hindsight bias*, also known as "I knew it all along." After an event occurs, we want to believe we predicted the outcome of that event before it actually happened. Our memory of the past seems more obvious than our understanding of the event actually was at the time. This is because our memories are not an accurate account of history, but rather a collage of both factual and imagined details that create a seemingly real and complete memory.

In their article *We Never Saw It Coming*, Neal Roese and Kathleen Vohs wrote, "Psychological research has shown that hindsight bias gets bigger when people feel that they have a good explanation for what occurred.... Most people try to find a single, credible story to help make sense of particular big events in life, and hindsight bias is part of this quest for meaning." We are exceedingly susceptible to suggestion when reconstructing memories because of hindsight bias. We can leverage this bias by providing a viable alternative perspective or explanation for past occurrences. This is what I call the *case study approach*. Case studies provide proof of concept for your position or idea because it is difficult for people to argue against past results—even when *you* have shaped the narrative.

●●●●●

MOMENTARY LAPSE OF REASON:

Time Pressure

The contract with one of our largest customers was expiring soon. Leading up to our renegotiating meeting, the customer account manager, the vice president of our division and I worked for weeks on our new proposal. We even took a negotiation class together to ensure our strategy was rock solid.

Our customer had canceled several meetings with us to discuss the new contract. Both the account manager and VP were getting antsy as we approached the end of the contract. If it expired our customer would surely open negotiations with our largest competitor and we desperately needed that business to make our numbers.

Our customer was in a great mood when we finally met to present our proposal. As the marketing guy, my role was to walk her through the presentation deck. It was a thorough accounting of all the things we had accomplished together over the course of the previous contract. At the end of the presentation, the account manager would go over the details of the new contract. As we had learned in negotiation training, our offer was close to the bare minimum of what we were willing to provide. This allowed us room to negotiate. Our goal was to set the anchor of the negotiation and eventually wind up in the middle of our range of acceptability.

The presentation was roughly an hour long. Our customer seemed impressed with all that we had accomplished together. She was very complimentary. At the end of the presentation, the account manager proposed the new deal. It took him all of two minutes to cover the major points. We were fully prepared for her counter offer.

No sooner had he finished the last point, our VP spoke up for the first time in the meeting: "Oh, and we are also prepared to offer you...." And the VP blurted out all of the items we had saved for the counter offers. All of them.

I believe my jaw hit the table. The client (who was still looking at the deal summary page when the VP threw the kitchen sink at her) looked up with a straight face and said, "I'll take it!" Just like that, we had given her the worst possible deal for our company.

So, what happened here?

Our VP choked on the time pressure. The client knew we needed to close this deal by a certain date, so she postponed the negotiation until the very last minute. The time pressure really affected our VP's ability to think rationally, so the customer was given everything she wanted (and then some) without a single round of negotiation.

Time pressure often brings out the worst in our thinking. Why do you think television game shows employ time pressure? It makes for more interesting viewing when contestants shift into autopilot and give ridiculous answers or freeze altogether. Time pressure makes even the smartest contestants say the silliest things.

When reflective and rational thought is restricted by time pressure, we are more easily affected by subtle cues that lead us to impulse decisions. That's what happened to our VP and, if you are human, it has happened to you, too.

If you are feeling pressured to make a decision, remember: time is money, and they who control the timetable usually get the money. Take the time to make better decisions.

● ● ● ● ●

THE FIFTH DEADLY SIN
DOUBLING DOWN:
Throwing Good Money After Bad

Persistence. Determination. Grit. These are all highly valued traits, and for good reason: success takes perseverance. But sometimes, the effort, time, or money we've already spent prevents us from seeing when it's time to change course. Instead, we "double down," throwing good money after bad, holding on to legacy objects, ideas, and people despite ample reason to move on without them.

The Best Laid Plans

Retailers have a job function called merchandise planning. The primary responsibility of a planner is to determine how much of each product to produce, or buy from manufacturers, to sell in their stores or online. In essence, they predict how much of each product consumers will buy. Obviously, businesses lose money when they buy products that don't sell, but they also lose money when they run out of stock. Predicting consumer behavior is a difficult job, to say the least.

Years ago, I managed a project that required very specific sales data for a large retailer. The project sponsor, my client, informed me that the company had recently implemented sophisticated planning software that would provide me with the exact data that I needed in a matter of minutes. He had me work with the Director of Merchandise Planning. I'll call her Sue.

Sue was a conservatively dressed, detail oriented woman in her late 30's. She was friendly, but not prone to idle chatter. Her posture was always perfect. Sue had a parental quality, her small team of planners often following her around like duck-lings. In short, she looked like someone who would have thoroughly vetted data at her fingertips.

Confident that my data request could be handled with a few keystrokes, I approached Sue with a laundry list of reporting needs. My request was met with an uncharacteristic look of sheer terror. Frankly, I was confused. It was my understanding that this information was easy to pull. When I said as much, Sue explained that she would have to gather the information "by hand" from printed reports, input the raw data into an Excel spreadsheet, then make the calculations I needed. That was her process. If she were actually engaged in planning for the company, she would then upload the results—again "by hand"—into the sophisticated planning program.

If that process doesn't make any sense to you, you're in good company. I did a little probing. Sue revealed that the new planning program was so difficult to use, she had determined it was more efficient for her team to plan the old way and fake compliance. The planners had voiced their concerns about the system when it was implemented. When nothing was done to address their complaints, they adapted to their circumstances and did what they were told—sort of. Actually, they just stopped complaining and developed a workaround, inputting barely enough data to make it look as if they were using the new program. Essentially, the sophisticated system almost doubled their workload. I couldn't imagine a less productive process.

It took Sue a few days to provide the information I needed; to her credit, the information was vetted thoroughly. I finished the project and presented my report to the client, who was pleased with the result. It is quite easy for a leader of a large business to become disconnected with what is going on in the field because intimidated subordinates often tell the boss what he wants to hear instead of the truth. I thought my client should know what is happening in his organization so, at the conclusion of my presentation, I mentioned how unproductive the planning system was and that it was a source of frustration with the entire planning team.

His response shocked me. He said, "We paid over a million dollars for that system. It's not going anywhere. They will just have to learn to use it. Maybe I'll pay for some more training." I was surprised because this was a highly successful, intelligent, well-educated man, but he simply could not see the flaw in his reasoning.

The million dollars they paid for the sophisticated system should not have been a factor in his decision. That money was a *sunk cost*: it was gone no matter what he decided to do next. His only concern should have been what was best for the company going forward, and he would never be free to see all his options as long as he was blinded by that million dollars lost.

We often hold on to things beyond their utility, and sometimes that loyalty to objects, systems, ideas, even people can negatively influence our decision-making process. Frankly, it's hard to let go. There are many reasons for this. First, we all bear the accountability and ownership of our previous decisions, which feel like direct reflections of us as individuals. We don't want to admit we were wrong; we might be replaced as decision makers due to that "bad" choice. Second, we tend to become emotionally attached to both people and things. Letting go often means feeling a sense of loss and we are inclined to avoid loss more than we value gain (more on that in the chapter on risk aversion). Third, as we have already established, human beings loathe change. Letting go of something disturbs the status quo and, to many of us, that is a frightening proposition.

Fear is a mighty motivator. Separation can cause great anxiety, and taking a shot to the ego can feel catastrophic. This is why our natural fear of humiliation—or *ego-death*—is the primary weapon of bullies. We human beings protect our outer image with our lives because we need connection and group approval. Perhaps every example of doubling down has at least a little fear of ego death embedded in it. Doubling down does not mean you are a hoarder or clingy person; it simply means you carry the same unconscious fears as the rest of us.

Ultimately, my client's efficiency objective was to establish a planning system that would give him the most productivity for the least amount of money. His leadership objective was to establish an environment in which his planners would thrive, both personally and professionally. Forcing his teams to work with a useless software program accomplished neither objective, regardless of the original investment or intent. From a decision-making standpoint, my client's choice should have been the answer to this question: What is best for the organization moving forward?

For the record, I'm not sure which choice my client made, but I hope he did something to improve the process for those overworked planners. We cannot change the past, but we can shape the future.

The Sinking Lineup

The sunk cost fallacy is often seen in the business of sports, particularly those featuring guaranteed player contracts. A guaranteed contract represents a sunk cost to the team the minute it is signed: the team must pay the full amount of the contract regardless of the player's performance or physical ability to play. Tens of millions of dollars in "dead money" is spent every season on players who do not contribute to the team's success.

The professional sports industry is a competitive business both on and off the field. A general manager's primary responsibility is to put together a winning team to compete not only against other teams, but also against other forms of entertainment for their fans' discretionary dollar. In general, it makes sense to lure in talented free-agent players with long, expensive contracts. However, there are myriad examples of teams signing hot players to these types of contracts, only to see the player get hurt or mysteriously underperform on the field.

In 2013, the Atlanta Braves signed center fielder B.J. Upton to a five-year, $72 million dollar guaranteed contract. Upton was considered a five-tool player out of high school and he had been a first-round draft pick (second overall) of the Tampa Bay Rays in 2002. He produced in the major leagues for eight seasons, stealing more than 40 bases in three consecutive seasons and hitting seven home runs in the 2008 playoffs. In case you are not a baseball fan, those are impressive statistics. In 2013, when the Atlanta Braves signed him to a contract, he was a sought-after free agent in the prime of his baseball career.

In the same off-season, the Braves' general manager Frank Wren traded for B.J.'s younger brother, Justin Upton. The interest in the Upton brothers made sense for the Braves. They were both power-hitting outfielders, and the Braves' long-time clutch power hitter, Chipper Jones, had just retired. The novelty of signing brothers to play in the same outfield attracted a great deal of attention for the team and interest from fans. Some predicted the Braves outfield would be the best in baseball, both offensively and defensively.

Unfortunately, things didn't go as planned. While Justin played well, B.J. struggled mightily. He played poorly at the beginning of the season and things snowballed from there. For the season, he hit only .184, which is terrible by baseball standards for a starting position player. His home run total was a third of what it had been in 2012, and he hit less than half the doubles he had the previous year. To make matters worse, he was striking out at a higher rate. His production was historically bad and it was hard to watch.

The Braves had a dilemma. They were paying B.J. $12 million, which was the second highest salary on the team, but his performance was hurting the ball club. All baseball players go through slumps, but few slumps last all season. Like all professionals, B.J. wanted to keep playing to improve his game: the best way to pull out of a slump is to play. By all accounts B.J. worked hard, but nothing seemed to help.

Local sports talk show hosts and fans were of the opinion that the Braves "had" to play B.J. because they were paying him so much. The Braves were obviously of the same opinion because they allowed him to play consistently until the playoffs, when the decision was finally made to pull him out of the lineup.

The Braves' organizational objective had been to put a winning team on the field. Just like the cost of my client's bad planning system, the players' salaries are irrelevant once the season begins. It may be embarrassing for a general manager to admit to a poor decision, but they should have acknowledged B.J.'s salary as a sunk cost and fielded the most productive nine players every game to maximize their chances of winning.

B.J.'s contract was a notably bad one and cost Braves general manager Frank Wren his job. I can't help but wonder what would have happened if the club had decided to "eat" the contract and sit the unproductive player. Had the Braves played their best performing players instead of their highest paid ones, would they have won more games and saved the general manager's job? Success solves a lot of problems. Had they taken that approach, B.J.'s contract might have been relegated to an embarrassing footnote in an otherwise successful season. Instead, it became the key factor in the Braves underperforming that season and the general manager was replaced.

Ponzi's Pyramid

In 1920, Charles Ponzi was a 38-year-old Italian immigrant who worked in his father-in-law's grocery store. His life and career had been both adventurous and unfortunate. He had been a bank manager, a sign painter, a clerk, a translator... and had served two stints in prison. He had wandered all over the United States and Canada before settling down in Boston, where he would launch the most infamous "rob Peter to pay Paul" schemes in financial history. It was so audacious that this type of fraudulent endeavor would forever bear his name—a Ponzi Scheme.

How did Charles Ponzi wind up as the poster boy of financial impropriety? Well, his misfortunes were largely due to his unbridled belief that it was his aristocratic birthright to live the lavish lifestyle of the privileged.

Carlo Pietro Giovanni Guglielmo Tebaldo Ponzi was born on March 3, 1882 in Lugo, Italy. His father was a postman and the Ponzi family lived a middle-class lifestyle. However, Carlo's grandparents on his mother's side held the titles Don and Donna, which meant they were members of the aristocracy. He was an only child and pampered by his mother. She yearned for him to reestablish the family's social rank and planted that seed in young Carlo's mind. He would spend much of his life trying to make that dream a reality.

Carlo was an intelligent child and good student, so his mother sent him to college at the University of Rome, funded by a small inheritance from his late father. Filled with stories of his aristocratic relatives, he began running with a group of wealthy students and living well above his means. These distractions prevented him from achieving any level of academic success. He eventually left Rome with neither a diploma nor his inheritance. Ponzi's uncle encouraged the dropout to go to America where "the streets are paved with gold."

On November 17, 1903, the *SS Vancouver* docked in Boston Harbor and Carlo got his first taste of the new world. On the two-week voyage,

Carlo lost most of his travel budget gambling. When he walked off the ship, he was nearly penniless. As Mitchell Zuckoff wrote in his book *Ponzi's Scheme*, "He spoke no English, had no marketable skills, and considered it a source of pride that he had never worked a day in his life." He spent the next four years drifting, working what he considered to be menial jobs, and living hand-to-mouth. He became fluent in English and changed his name to Charles.

In 1907, he moved to Montreal, Canada where he found work as a clerk at a bank that catered to Italian immigrants, Banco Zarossi. The bank's founder, Luigi Zarossi, offered an unheard-of 6% return on deposits.

The business model used by Banco Zarossi's competitors was to buy Italian securities paying 3%, give 2% to their depositors, and retain a modest 1% return for the bank. Zarossi's math simply didn't add up. There was no way for him to purchase an Italian security with a 3% return, then deliver a 6% return to depositors. It was a scam, of course, a classic "rob Peter to pay Paul" scheme in which new deposits were used to pay the older depositors' interest.

Less than a year after Ponzi began working at the bank, Zarossi stuffed a bag full of depositor money and escaped to Mexico, leaving his family and the business behind. The bank folded, and Ponzi was once again out of work.

On August 29, 1908 Ponzi stole a blank check out of the checkbook of a former bank client, the Canadian Warehousing Company. He cashed the check at another bank in the amount of $423.58 and went on a shopping spree for new fine clothing. He was quickly caught by a Montreal detective and served twenty months in prison.

Shortly after he left prison, Charles decided to move back to the United States because his reputa-tion in Montreal was ruined. Unfortunately, he was arrested at the border for smuggling illegal immigrants into the country and spent another two years in prison.

After leaving prison for the second time, Ponzi managed to land a job at the Wichita Falls Motor Company, which manufactured flatbed trucks and sold them around the world. Charles put his language skills to use in the foreign sales department. There he learned about foreign currencies, exchange rates, shipping routes, tariffs, and postal fees. This valuable information would come to serve him well.

By 1920, Charles Ponzi had settled in Boston, a middle aged married man working in his father-in-law's grocery store. He had not restored his family's aristocratic lifestyle, but always felt there was still hope. His wife complained that he constantly spent time devising ways to get rich quick, and one day, Ponzi hit what seemed to be the jackpot.

In the early 1900's, every country had its own postal regulations and currency, so sending someone in a different country a stamped, self-addressed envelope for a reply message was nearly impossible. This was obviously a detriment to international business concerns. So, in 1906, a system of postal currency called International Reply Coupons was created in 63 developed countries to make it easier to mail letters and packages between independent countries. These coupons held a fixed value from one country to another and could be redeemed for stamps in any post office of the 63 member countries.

After WWI, some economies (including Italy's) collapsed, and their currency lost value compared to the U.S. dollar. Ponzi realized that he could buy International Reply Coupons in Italy, using Italy's devalued currency, and redeem them for postal stamps in the United States for the much more valuable U.S. dollar. In fact, by his calculation, each transaction would generate a 230% profit before expenses. The post office wouldn't allow him to redeem large amounts of International Reply Coupons for money, so his plan was to buy U.S. postage stamps using the coupons purchased with cheaper foreign currency, and then sell them at a discount to businesses that had regular transactions overseas. The companies would benefit from saving money on postage, and he would make a healthy profit on the difference. It appeared to be a legitimate opportunity and he would be the first to exploit it.

When Ponzi came up with his coupon exchange investment idea, he formed the Securities Exchange Company and set up shop at 27 School Street in Boston, Massachusetts. He didn't have any money to buy International Reply Coupons, so he began looking for investors. The "investment" opportunity was simple: investors would give Ponzi their money and receive a receipt or "Ponzi note" in return. At the end of 45 days, the investor could exchange the note for their full investment amount plus a 50% return, or the investor could let it ride for a full three months and double the original investment. At the time, banks offered an annual return of approximately 5%. On top of that, banks were risky: in the 1920s, there was no FDIC to insure your bank deposits. If the bank went under, your money went with it. Ponzi's deal seemed like a wonderful alternative.

To inspire investors, Ponzi convinced a respected local Italian grocer named Ettore Giberti to sell the Ponzi notes for a 10% commission. Giberti bought $10 of Ponzi notes so he could say he was an actual investor. Giberti promoted the coupons with his customers, giving Ponzi's scheme instant credibility.

When he paid his first coupon redemption, word spread fast in the Italian community that Charles Ponzi had a legitimate investment opportunity and the floodgates opened. Ponzi's investors were not only the poor and undereducated. Seemingly everyone wanted to invest in Ponzi's scheme, including government officials, members of the police department, newspaper employees, and business leaders. Ponzi notes seemed too good to be true. As it turned out, they were.

As investment money began rolling in, Ponzi went to work on the operations of his new venture. He had a friend buy some coupons in Italy and ship them to Boston, but he struggled to find a buyer. Companies were not interested in buying discount postage stamps from this enthusiastic little man. By the time Ponzi figured out there was no market for his idea, investors were literally lined up at his office ready to give him their money.

If we believe that his original intention had been to run a legitimate business, Ponzi faced a difficult decision at this point. He could have simply returned the early investors' money and gone out of business. It would have been messy, but businesses and investments fail all the time.

Unfortunately for him and his victims, he decided to double down on his scheme. We may never know why, but we do know that, in his mind, he was always one move away from living the lavish lifestyle he was intended to live. Perhaps he finally saw his chance to restore his royal bloodline to respectability.

Ponzi took in over $20 million in 1920, more than $220 million in current dollar value. The average annual household income at the time was only around $2,000. It was quite a jump from grocery clerk to financial mogul in less than a year. In a way, Carlo achieved his mother's dream of living the life of an aristocrat, but it was short-lived. He formed the Securities Exchange Company in January of 1920 and turned himself in to authorities in August 1920. His aristocrat lifestyle only lasted eight months. He spent nearly eight years in prison and was deported back to Italy upon parole. With a few more calamitous adventures under his belt, Charles Ponzi died in 1948 in Rio de Janeiro with only $75 to his name.

Flight of the Concorde

The Concorde is still regarded as a technological wonder in aviation. As a supersonic, turbojet-powered aircraft flying at 60,000 feet and reaching speeds of Mach 2.04, it could take passengers from New York to Paris in three and a half hours—less than half the time it took a conventional jet-powered aircraft to fly the same route. You could fly to LA for brunch and be home in New York by dinner. In addition to its speed, the Concorde was a luxury jet, so passengers flew in style.

The Concorde introduced the aviation industry to two technological breakthroughs: computer-controlled engine air intakes and carbon-fiber brakes. The air intake innovation allowed the plane to fly at high speeds without blowing the engines apart, and carbon-fiber brakes would eventually become the norm in the industry. Jock Lowe, the Concorde's longest-serving pilot, said it had so much power, yet was so maneuverable, that even ex-fighter pilots had to get used to it. The jet was simply an aviation innovation marvel.

All that advanced technology must have led to an expensive ticket, right? According to Michael Gebicki of Traveller.com, "A ticket cost roughly the same as a first-class seat on a conventional aircraft." The question is, with such an impressive list of features and benefits to travelers, what happened to the Concorde?

Let's start at the beginning. The Concorde was a joint venture between French aircraft manufacturer Aerospatiale and an English company named British Aircraft Corporation. Together, they built twenty Concordes, which were operated by Air France and British Airways. To make the deal financially feasible, the French and British governments provided massive subsidies for these airline companies to purchase the jets. After all, this aviation technology was a source of national pride, far exceeding anything the United States or the Soviet Union had developed. With the fanfare befitting such an exciting and innovative advancement in aviation, flight service began in 1976.

The Concorde immediately faced two challenges: fuel costs and noise pollution. When the joint project began, aviation fuel was relatively cheap. However, the oil crisis of the 1970's made the supersonic jets extremely expensive to operate. The bigger problem, though, was noise pollution. The Concorde's speed created a sonic boom. While the Concorde initially flew routes all over the world, noise complaints put a damper on this new technology. The uproar led to governments restricting the planes' flight over land areas. Soon after its introduction, the Concorde would only be permitted to fly transatlantic routes, which reduced its market viability. Its stops were reduced to London, Paris, and New York. In essence, the jet's greatest asset became a liability.

British Airways and Air France operated the Concorde for nearly 27 years and reportedly did return a profit. However, as the planes approached 30 years of service, they needed updates to the systems on board, which would have required a substantial investment. Given the rising costs of maintaining these aging planes, and the post-9/11 slump in the travel market, the companies chose not to make the investment needed to keep the Concorde in service. On April 10, 2003, both Air France and British Airways announced they would retire the Concorde.

Some people believed the Concorde was grounded because the English and French governments ended subsidies supporting luxury travel for the rich and famous. Others believed it was the public relations nightmare that ensued after the Air France Concorde flight 4590 crash in 2000. The plane ran over a piece of debris on the runway that punctured a tire on the landing gear. The tire exploded under the weight of the plane and ignited a fire, which caused two of the engines to fail. While the crash had nothing to do with the maintenance and operation of the plane, it cast doubt on the safety of the Concorde.

When I began researching this story, I fully expected to find an example of how politics and the egos of big-company executives kept money pouring into the Concorde for the glory of the brand, but I was wrong. That's not what happened. In the end, it appeared to be a rational business decision to avoid an investment that would yield them a poor return. They wisely avoided the pitfalls of the dreaded double down.

The Concorde was such an impressive aircraft. I personally hope it makes a triumphant return, but I wouldn't bet on it. Sometimes bigger, better, faster, stronger isn't viable. Smart decision makers know when to say when.

On the Flip Side of Doubling Down

Whether you were aware of it or not, you have been on the wrong end of a double down decision at some point in your life. Either you have factored in a sunk cost variable in an important decision, or someone else has and that mistake had a negative impact on you.

Now that you are aware of this deadly sin of decision making with regard to your own thought process, let's examine how you can apply this knowledge to influence the decisions of others. There are times when we need people to double down and other times when we need them to avoid it. Here are a few tactics to consider:

Diminish the value of the sunk cost. When a sunk cost is preventing someone from moving on and you need them to avoid doubling down, diminish the perceived value of the sunk cost. Think of it as a variable in a decision equation. When the sunk cost variable has less value, the other variables (hopefully more pertinent to the decision) take on greater value, which leads to a better decision. When we accept that something is not worth having, it is easier for us to move forward without it. It makes the decision much less complicated.

There are two approaches to diminish the value of something: reduce its perceived worth, or make it appear easy to attain.

B.J. Upton's worth to the team was really his contribution on the field, not his salary. His contribution was minimal for the Braves in 2013;

therefore, the Braves front office should have decided to play a more "valuable" player.

Remember the Members Only jacket story from the Justification chapter? Had my father asked me to wait until after Christmas to buy the jacket, I wouldn't have wanted it. The appeal of the jacket diminished when everyone else had one. It was too easy to acquire. Everyone was a member of the club.

Remind them of the (sunk) cost. The real value we place on a sunk cost should be zero. However, in some situations there is value in maintaining the status quo. If this is the case, remind the decision maker of the *cost* of the thing they want to replace... and do it publicly. That nudge should be enough to drag the sunk cost into the equation making any new action seem *more* expensive. That's usually too much for a decision maker to accept.

We also place a higher value on those things for which we had to work hard to attain. This is the *power of extra effort.* The extra trouble or pain that we must endure in order to get or achieve something adds value to it. That's why "playing hard to get" is so alluring. All that extra effort required by the suitor adds value to the pursued. When you want someone to value something, remind him or her how difficult it was to attain or implement. In other words, get them to factor in all aspects of the sunk cost.

How could you have known? This justification deflects blame away from a decision maker's earlier, failed decision, freeing them from responsibility and allowing them to move on rather than trying to save the original decision.

This technique can be effective in part because it is associated with *actor-observer bias,* whereby we attribute our own actions to external factors, while attributing others' behavior to internal factors. When you want someone to move on, find reasons why they are not to blame for early failures or poor decisions. Deflect, deflect, deflect.

Publicly remind them of their beliefs. When you want someone to double down, publicly remind them of *why* they made the original decision in the first place. This employs the concept of *belief perseverance,* which is the tendency to reject rational evidence disproving a belief and becoming even more doggedly insistent on its validity when the belief has been announced publicly. People will often dig in on their faulty beliefs even when proven wrong. The effect is more pronounced when there is greater emotional attachment to the subject, or when the belief or decision is tied to one's self-identity.

• • • • •

MOMENTARY LAPSE OF REASON:

Emotional Arousal

He didn't fit the mold of a violent criminal. He was a seemingly normal, mild-mannered, law abiding citizen... when one day, in a fit of rage, he snapped and did the unthinkable.

How could this happen? In his confession to the authorities, he described the event as an out-of-body experience. He also used the term "autopilot" to explain his thought process and behavior. It was a crime of passion driven by rage.

If this story sounds familiar, it's because it is. While the story above is a recent one, there have been songs, poems, articles, books (both fiction and nonfiction) and countless studies done about crimes of passion. By definition, a crime of passion is committed against someone the perpetrator loves, which is the great irony of the crime. Generally, there has been a falling out. By committing the crime, the perpetrator destroys any chance of reconciliation. In other words, success guarantees failure. It is the pinnacle of irrational thinking.

This, of course, is an extreme example of when emotional arousal triggers one's autopilot cognitive processing system, but our emotions affect our decision making on a daily basis.

In fact, fMRI neuro-imagery reveals that when choosing one brand over another, consumers mostly use emotions as opposed to analyzing product information. And when we are in a hot emotional state, we are compelled to satisfy our immediate desires, even at the expense of long-term goals. Snickers leveraged this concept with their *Hangry* advertising campaign.

Retail therapy is real. Extremes of mood tend to trigger autopilot thinking, which can lead to compulsive and impulsive behavior, leaving us susceptible to influence tactics. Shoppers in an extremely negative mood do feel a temporary positive effect from compulsive shopping. Unfortunately, this is an example of meeting an immediate need (self-soothing) at the expense of long-term consequences (financial distress).

On the other hand, theme parks go out of their way to create a sense of euphoria for their visitors. They want us in an exuberant mood, so they feature bright colors, happy music, and cheery and nostalgic characters greeting guests on the streets. Speaking from experience, these tactics work. I can't leave a theme park without wondering what happened to my money. Of course, I had happily handed it over, readily acknowledging a splurge for the occasion. It felt so good at the time.

Emotions influence how we think and behave. We unconsciously draw on our emotions from similar experiences in the past, and they sway our preferences and influence our decisions. Storytelling is such a popular marketing concept because companies want their customers to form emotional connections with their products. And the stories that create a state of emotional arousal are most likely to trigger a momentary lapse of reason.

THE SIXTH DEADLY SIN

INFLEXIBILITY: Believing There is
One Right Way to do Everything

Flexibility is a commendable trait... especially in others! Because the truth is, to be flexible means admitting our earlier opinions, assessments, or decisions might have been wrong, and we hate doing that. Flexibility takes work; if it puts us at odds with longstanding biases, it can take tremendous courage.

As we have established, we human beings love consistency and predictability. When we encounter something or someone for the first time, our brains unconsciously categorizes them, building the heuristics our autopilot thinking will need later. Once we have tucked that person or thing into our usual pigeonholes, *confirmatory bias* tries to keep us on autopilot by ignoring any contradictory evidence. That's why first impressions are so important. Once someone has put you into a category, it is extremely difficult to change that person's opinion of you.

Inflexibility employs the cognitive bias called *functional fixedness*. We only see one way to do something or use something. The more extreme manifestation of inflexibility is "black or white" or "all or nothing" thinking. This approach is counter-productive in business and other facets of life. We all know someone who touts, "it's my way or the highway." And we hate working with them.

The obvious application of inflexibility is with regard to process. Many of us have rigid methods for doing things. We find comfort in our systems and approaches. This gets back to consistency and predictability. Technology has forced us to reevaluate and often update our legacy processes... although I still balance my checkbook by hand. Let's face it, it's difficult to step out of our comfort zone and try a different method or technique.

If the Panties Fit

At one point in my career, I managed the brand-growth strategies for a large intimate apparel retailer. Our team was extremely dedicated and constantly tested ideas to improve every aspect of the business. We had a formal growth plan, but good ideas can come from anywhere. So, I regularly met with team members from every area of the business and every job grade level to receive feedback and listen to their ideas. It amazed me how creative they were. In fact, one of our most brilliant new product ideas came from a summer intern.

We also sought regular feedback from our clientele. We invested in focus groups, personal interviews, panel discussions, and secondary research from outside firms. We also interviewed store employees, observed shopping patterns, and tested new products. It was often said around the office that we knew our customer better than she knew herself. Often said, but not always true.

All this research led us to a new product opportunity. Our designers combined three of our customers' favorite features into one panty. The product was made with a light, stretchy material that made it more comfortable to wear. It featured a synthetic fabric, which provided cooling, perspiration-wicking properties on hot days. Finally, it had no seams, which prevented seam lines from showing through pants. We all believed this new product was a no-brainer home run. The only question was how fast could we get it to market?

The product was manufactured and rolled into stores with great anticipation. It was merchandised with our other panty offerings on a large table placed in the center of the store right in front of the entrance. Like our other panties, it was offered as a price-multiple, meaning the customer received a deep discount for buying a certain number of pairs at once. This product was sure to take our panty sales to the next level.

And yet the sound we heard was crickets. Nothing. The product was dying on the vine and that made no sense. "But the research said this would work..." are the famous last words of the classic marketer as he is escorted out the door.

Why wasn't this product selling? We made a wonderful product based on our knowledge of the customers' lifestyle, and, the planners were threatening to pull the plug. Business was business, after all.

I begged for a little time and visited a few stores in various parts of the country. Our sales data revealed that the only store locations where the product sold well were those in southern states. They were popular in areas with a warm, humid climate, like Texas and Florida. When I talked to the store sales staff, they raved about the product for all the reasons we believed it would be popular across the country.

Then it hit me. Of course they raved about it in the South: the product was perfect for their climate. If we wanted the product to take off in cold climates, we had to associate it with energetic activities.

Our hottest selling pants at the time were yoga pants. They were snug but flexible and originally designed for working out. But we knew better. Our customer was wearing them everywhere, typically as a replacement for jeans or sweat pants.

The pants were very comfortable, but also a bit revealing; panty lines showed right through. Because they were seamless, our new panties were the ideal underwear for yoga pants. Because they were less revealing, our customer could wear them out running errands; because they were breathable, she could wear them to the gym; and because they were light and stretchy, they were comfortable to wear lounging at home.

When I returned to the office, I shared my crazy idea. "Before we pull this product, let's try something different," I told the planners. We took the product off the price-multiple table. We replaced the price tags, nearly doubling the price. Then we found a new display for them adjacent to our yoga pants. Finally, we renamed the product "The Yoga Panty" and described its three differentiating attributes. It worked. Unit sales went through the roof—even at the higher price point.

Our changes improved product sales for two reasons. One reason was *adjacency*, when one product is placed next to another related or complementary product. In this case, we leveraged a yoga pant adjacency to draft off that product's popularity and showcase the functionality of our new panty. In his book *Why We Buy*, Paco Underhill wrote, "placing one item next to another creates some spark and sells more of one or even both. Adjacencies are also about order—coming up with a sensible sequence of things." He was right. These small tweaks helped a wonderful product succeed in the marketplace.

The second reason was *functional fixedness*, a bias that prevents us from seeing a full range of options and impairs our ability to think of novel solutions to problems. We broke the functional fixedness bias in our customer's mind by creating a new use for the product. More importantly, we broke our own functional fixedness about how we merchandised the panty category. We had been stuck in our belief that there was one right way to sell this product because the product had only one function. It's amazing what can happen when we break through the decision-making sin of inflexibility.

Do They Know It's Christmas?

On July 13, 1985, one of the greatest global musical charity events occurred simultaneously at Wembley stadium in London, England, and John F. Kennedy Stadium in Philadelphia, Pennsylvania. Live Aid was the ambitious undertaking of musicians Bob Geldof and Midge Ure, who were moved by a television report on the famine crisis in Ethiopia. The concert was dubbed "The Global Jukebox," and for good reason. As a huge music fan,

I remember watching the broadcast in awe of the collection of popular artists from seemingly every genre of music at the time. It was a music lover's dream. I also remember feeling like I was participating in something very special, something global, from my living room sofa.

The story begins when Geldof and Ure wrote the song, *Do They Know It's Christmas?* The pair formed a super group of popular musicians in the UK to record the song with the proceeds going to organizations supporting relief in Africa. They called this charitable organization Band Aid and released the single in December 1984. It was a catchy yet poignant pop song, but more importantly the single raised millions for famine relief.

Following the success of *Do They Know It's Christmas*, a similar effort occurred in the United States by the group United Support of Artists (USA) for Africa. The song *We Are the World* was written by Michael Jackson and Lionel Richie and produced by Quincy Jones. The group recruited over 40 popular musicians to record the track. That single was released in March of 1985 and along with merchandising sales reportedly raised over 60 million dollars for charity.

Encouraged by the success of the two hit charitable music releases, Geldof and Ure decided to broadcast a concert around the world to promote donations. It would be called Live Aid. If two songs could raise tens of millions of dollars for charity, how much could a globally televised event raise?

So many artists wanted to participate that Geldof had to turn many down. Each band only had about seventeen minutes to perform their set. David Bowie "donated" some of his time for an emotionally moving video about the realities of famine in Africa. Bowie's donation of time was a precious gift as the video reportedly drove a huge bump in donations. As a teenager at the time, I was moved by the music, I was moved by the charity, I was moved by the event. Live Aid left an impression on me.

In the end, around 1.9 billion people watched Live Aid in 150 countries. Promoters reported raising $140 million in donations. Not only were Geldof and crew able to pull off one of the most amazing global broadcasting event of the era, they managed dozens of big egos at two day-long concerts attended by over 150,000 fans. They also raised a staggering amount of money to help people struggling to get the basic necessities of life. It was the right thing to do, wasn't it?

Ethiopia was the third poorest country in the world at the time of the Live Aid concert. This landlocked African nation was historically plagued by drought leading to starvation. When Geldof and Band Aid began collecting charitable donations and providing relief for Ethiopia, its people were experiencing a humanitarian crisis. While drought was a factor, the crisis was actually man-made.

A communist military junta called the Derg had run the Ethiopian government since 1974. Their ruthless leader was Mengistu Haile Mariam. While the Ethiopian people were starving, this violent despot threw an extravagant $200 million celebration to commemorate the overthrow of the previous regime of Haile Selassie. Much of the money used for the lavish inauguration celebration of Mengistu's Communist Workers Party was diverted from aid intended to relieve famine victims.

By the early 1980's, Mengistu's government was fighting various opposing factions. To control his citizens and battle these groups of insurgents, Mengistu enlisted the help of Russia. Much of the money and supplies provided by relief agencies were redirected to acquire sophisticated weapons from Mengistu's new ally. Soon Ethiopia, whose population was literally starving, had the largest standing army in Africa.

With Russia's help, the Derg forced tribes off their traditional land, burned farms, destroyed crops, and killed livestock to starve the Ethiopian people. In addition to murder and torture, the Derg also terrorized citizens by using chemical weapons, nerve gas, and napalm on starving noncombatants. Then, by offering food and safety, Mengistu's troops coerced them into either joining the military or relocating to camps on the other side of the country. Hungry and desperate, millions of Ethiopian citizens were forced to leave their homelands in resettlement marches to refugee camps. It was reported at the time that 100,000 people died in the process.

Drought was a historically common reason for famine in Ethiopia, but it wasn't the main source of misery in the country at that time. In the year after Live Aid, over 100,000 tons of food was confiscated by the Ethiopian government and used to pay its military and the Russians. In essence, hunger relief resources went to fund the groups who were slaughtering innocent people and causing much of the suffering, rather than feeding the hungry.

Surely Geldof and the Live Aid organizers were unaware of Mengistu's human rights violations, the inhumane practices of the Ethiopian government, and their theft of millions of dollars in humanitarian aid?

Quite the contrary. Geldof and company knew exactly what was going on in Ethiopia. A Spin Magazine article titled *Live Aid: The Terrible Truth,* published in July, 1986, exposed this story to the world. Spin Magazine was demonized for the report by other news organizations, but eventually investigative reporters substantiated Spin's story. According to Bob Guccione Jr., founder of Spin Magazine, "Geldof was warned, repeatedly, from the outset by several relief agencies in the field about Mengistu, who was dismantling tribes, mercilessly conducting resettlement marches on which 100,000 people died, and butchering helpless people." Geldof's response was: "I'll shake hands with the Devil on my left and on my right to get to the people we are meant to help."

Unfortunately, according to sources much of the charitable donations provided by the Live Aid effort did not get to the people they were meant to help. They wound up paying for the ruthless tactics of Mengistu, leading to the suffering of millions of Ethiopians.

I truly believe the motivations of Geldof and the administrators of Live Aid were pure and altruistic. People were starving. Food was plentiful around the world. The notion was to simply get the food to the people. That sounds reasonable. In fact, it felt unacceptable to do nothing when people were suffering and aid was readily available.

The problem is that charities don't always follow the Latin expression associated with the Hippocratic oath: Primum non nocere (above all, do no harm). Donating vast amounts of money and resources didn't solve the problem in Ethiopia—it exacerbated it. Yes, the Ethiopian people needed food and supplies, but handing these resources over to a tyrant was a terrible idea. Anthropologist Bonnie Holcomb said of the situation at the time, "I take the position that aid should be stopped until the situation can be turned around.... More lives can be saved by stopping aid."

Geldof had choices. He could have waited until a system was in place to ensure the aid went directly to the Ethiopian people. The proceeds from Live Aid could have funded relief in other areas of the world with more receptive political circumstances. He could have waited until the Derg regime fell out of power. The worst thing Geldof and his organization could have done was to hand the relief resources over to Mengistu's henchmen. Which is exactly what they did, because he could not see past his concept of moving the aid into Ethiopia as quickly as possible. As a result, Geldof's *inflexibility* contributed to the suffering of millions.

A few years after these events, Russian leader Mikhail Gorbachev introduced glasnost to the Soviet Union and the Russians, suffering from their own economic distress, stopped supporting the Mengistu government. By May of 1991, the Derg had crumbled. The Ethiopian People's Revolutionary Democratic Front took over and Mengistu fled to asylum in Zimbabwe. An Ethiopian court later convicted him of genocide and sentenced him to life in prison. As of this writing, Mengistu has not spent a day behind bars.

Sometimes we get stuck on an idea, or a system, or an approach. We become inflexible. Unfortunately, inflexibility can lead to disastrous results, like what occurred in Ethiopia. Be aware of and avoid the "my way or the highway" trap. There is a reason inflexibility is a deadly sin.

The Advantages of Color Blindness

My grandfather is a retired career navy man. He is straight out of central casting: big and barrel-chested with a shaved head and thick forearms. He's a gruff, old school, outdoorsman-type. Tough as nails. He is also color blind.

Colorblindness is considered a handicap, and it can prevent people from entering certain careers such as military pilot, electrician, or police officer. For the most part, however, colorblindness does not hinder people from pursuing most vocations. Actors, singers, lawyers, accountants, and even Presidents of the United States have been color-blind. Human beings have an amazing ability to adapt. One such case was Emerson Moser, senior crayon molder for Crayola. In his 37-year career he molded more than 1.4 billion crayons. Only after he retired did he reveal that he was blue-green color-blind.

When I was a kid, my grandfather shared stories of his experience in combat and the lessons he learned while fighting in Vietnam. He told me that our military used to fly soldiers with colorblindness over areas suspected of hiding enemy armaments and supplies—typically heavily wooded areas or thick brush. Militaries hid their equipment with camouflaged netting, making it difficult for people with perfect eyesight to detect. However, some colorblind soldiers could see right through the camouflage. My grandfather's "flawed" eyesight gave him a different perspective. And that perspective provided soldiers like him a distinct advantage when detecting the enemy hidden below.

We generally believe in what we see. Unfortunately, what we see is filtered through the lens of our perspective. Sometimes it takes another perspective to see what's hidden in plain sight. And sometimes that perspective comes from someone who sees the world differently—someone we believe to have "flawed" vision. When surrounded by people who share the same perspective, you are sure to miss something.

On a lighter note: My grandmother, a cheeky Australian with a wonderfully dry sense of humor, loved to dress my rough and tumble grandfather in soft pastels. When we were kids, my sister and I thought it hysterical to see him decked out in pinks and yellows and lavenders. He often looked like a contestant on the iconic television show *Dance Fever*. We tried to explain to him that he was dressed out of character, but he couldn't even comprehend what a soft pastel was or why it was out of character.

So, if you ever see a big, gruff looking guy lumbering around in a canary yellow outfit... that might be my grandfather. I didn't say colorblindness was an advantage in every aspect of life.

On the Flip Side of Inflexibility

As with each of the seven deadly sins of decision making, we all fit somewhere on the scale of inflexibility. Some of us are relatively flexible, while others are extremely inflexible. One's level of inflexibility typically depends on the topic at hand. We tend to be less flexible when we care deeply, and more flexible when we have less of a connection. In other words, the more we care, the less flexible we become. Some people are so inflexible that they are nearly impossible to deal with. Unfortunately, we cannot always probe for the level of "open-mindedness" with prospective colleagues or clients before agreeing to work with them. We have to learn to deal with them. So, how can we avoid being the victim of a "my way or the highway" person? Here are a few ideas:

Provide success stories. There is a level of risk aversion at play with regard to inflexibility. You might hear a "my way" person say, "Don't mess with success." But the world around us is constantly changing; failure to adjust is riskier than trying to sustain the old way of doing things. Holding on to the past is the path to obsolescence.

Sharing a success story about an alternative approach can be effective. Success stories leverage the power of social proof and they allay our risk aversion: it worked for him, so it can work for me. The known always has more credibility than the unknown. When we are uncertain, we feel more confident following an established path; a success story establishes one.

There is also the hurdle of the pride of author-ship that comes from developing a successful approach. You may hear: "*My* way works, so why change it?" When someone makes a statement like this, tread lightly. Avoid challenging someone's legacy process directly. That only serves to put them in a defensive frame of mind, which is unproductive. Rather, share your success story and let it germinate in Mr. My Way's mind. *He* has to come to the conclusion to change his process, on his own. The more you push, the more he will resist. Plant the seed and watch the idea grow. Then when the idea comes back around, congratu-late Mr. My Way on his brilliant new approach.

(Re)Write history. We saw this tactic in the *Familiarity* chapter and it works for inflexibility as well. We tend to remember the past as being better than it really was. This is called *rosy retrospection*. Whenever possible, frame your ideas with histori-cal references that support those ideas. By historical, I mean refer to the experiences of the

person or group that you are trying to influence: "Remember when we used this approach a few years ago and it worked so well (or it didn't work so well)?" This provides them with the context needed to connect and apply your idea with the current situation. It establishes a precedent, which is the "known" or familiar.

Frame the choices. By laying out the choices in a decision-making process, one can easily frame each choice in a positive or negative light. This tactic is more effective when you have historical references for each option. We are inclined to remember the choices we have made as being better than the options we rejected, regardless of the facts. This is called a *choice-supportive bias*. Use the positive halo of options chosen and the negative halo of rejected options to influence future decisions. This is why incumbents get elected at such a high rate. The incumbent is the known, while the challenger is the unknown. It supports our desire for consistency in that the decision was already made (at an earlier time). Why make a change now?

Adopt the Swiss army knife philosophy. This idea is really more about how to enhance *your* flexibility, rather than a tactic for influencing inflexible thinkers. The analogy here is simple: we are all like unique Swiss army knives equipped with a different set of tools. One of those tools may come in handy in an unexpected situation. Our potential goes largely untapped because the people around us do not realize or utilize all of our abilities, talents, and tools. One reason is inflexibility, but another is simply awareness. We are unaware of the abilities of others. Camouflage was a useful military tool until they discovered that soldiers with the colorblind "handicap" could often see right through it.

Inflexibility prevents us from recognizing the range of potential in others. This is a detriment to us because we don't use all of the tools at our disposal, including the talents and skills of the people around us. Improve your flexibility by getting to know people beyond their primary job function or the way you initially categorized them. Push yourself to explore different capabilities in others and catalog the tools in their toolbox. You'll never know when their "hidden" talents might prove useful.

• • • • •

MOMENTARY LAPSE OF REASON:

Fear

My first memory of public speaking came in the fifth grade. Each student was to present an oral book report to the class of about 30 kids. My report was on the book *The White Stag* by Kate Seredy. I thoroughly enjoyed the book and took pride in the report that I had written. Note cards were prepared with neatly handwritten notes, but they were only for backup. I was to memorize my entire presentation, word-for-word.

Standing in front of the class I managed to recite the first line or two of my report. Then my mind went blank. I couldn't remember what went next. I completely froze. My teacher encouraged me to check my notecards, but I was lost. The words on the cards no longer made any sense. There was an awkward and deafening silence in the room. The eyes of my classmates were burning my skin. My feet felt like they were nailed to the floor. I couldn't lift them, so I just shifted my weight from one leg to the other. The weight of my tiny body was unbearable. I was terrified and I just wanted to disappear.

In an attempt to help, the teacher asked all of the students to turn their desks around. The opposite happened. The sight of a room full of people with their backs to me was disturbing. I'll never forget that scene.

I apologized to the teacher and sat down without completing my report. For the next twenty years, I employed every tactic imaginable to avoid public speaking. And the longer I held out, the more fearful I became of the prospect. I was afraid of the memory of being afraid.

Years into my career it became readily apparent that my phobia was becoming a barrier to success. After reading self-help books and watching videos on the topic, I realized the only way to get over my fear of public speaking was to speak publicly. This revelation occurred around the same time that I began graduate school. The happy coincidence was that most of my graduate-level classes required oral presentations of some kind, so there would be ample opportunity to speak in public.

I took advantage of every uncomfortable opportunity to speak in class. Along the way, I learned a few tricks to make myself feel more comfortable in these situations and eventually the fear diminished. I declared myself "cured" when I was asked to give an unrehearsed speech in front of an audience of over 300 professionals. I turned the fear into anticipation and performed well on stage. The feedback I received from audience members was wonderful. That experience went a long way in building my confidence. Now I actually enjoy the rush of speaking. That said, please don't turn your backs on me during a speech. I can't promise that I'll be there when you turn back around.

Fear is a powerful, primal, instinctual emotion. It was essential to our survival when we were in danger of being eaten by predatory animals. Think of fear as a warning signal, without which we wouldn't be here today. Unfortunately, fear has no practical application in public speaking or other aspects of modern life. It unconsciously influences our thought processes and biases and ultimately impacts our behavior.

As Franklin D. Roosevelt said, "The only thing we have to fear, is fear itself." We all know that fear is a formidable emotion. Why is the fear of fear such a concern? Because we exhibit avoidance reflex reaction behavior at the mere memories of being afraid. I missed career opportunities because I avoided public speaking. I was afraid of being afraid. As Dr. Karl Albrecht explains, "Fear of fear probably causes more problems in our lives than fear itself."

Let's begin by looking at fear itself. What are we afraid of? Dr. Albrecht classifies fear into five categories:

- *Extinction*: The fear of death. This is the big one because our brains are wired primarily for the self-interest of survival.
- *Mutilation*: The fear of losing a body part or natural function. Survival is difficult enough

with a perfectly functioning body and mind, so obviously losing functionality can be a detriment to our chances of survival.

- *Loss of Autonomy*: The fear of being controlled by outside forces. We like to feel as if we have control over our circumstances. This is why the thought of being imprisoned or enslaved is such a terrifying notion.
- *Separation*: This is "the fear of abandonment, rejection, and loss of connectedness." This explains why being shunned or excommunicated is such a powerful punishment.
- *Ego death*: The fear of humiliation or loss of integrity. It elicits shame and self-disapproval.

Many of the seven deadly sins of decision making have a fear component. While we can't completely eliminate fear from life, we can learn techniques on how to deal with it. The first step is to identify which category of fear we are experiencing. This is important because some of the biggest decisions are made when we are feeling afraid. The next step is to challenge that fear with rational thought. Because fear is an autopilot trigger, we must counter that by activating our conscious mind to analyze the situation rationally.

Fear will often take us to the worst-case scenario, which typically has a low probability of occurring. Let your conscious mind explore the possibilities of positive outcomes and the rewards that come with them. Remember: the unbridled desire to succeed is far more powerful than the restrictive fear of failure.

THE SEVENTH DEADLY SIN
RISK AVERSION: When the Pain of Losing
Outweighs the Benefits of Gain

Opportunity Lost

In my early twenties, I worked for a regional advertising agency in Atlanta on relatively small, unexciting accounts. I dreamed of working for a global agency on more "sexy" accounts. That said, I had no complaints. I had a steady paycheck, I worked with good people, and I enjoyed a nice office overlooking the city. It was a comfortable life, just not the one of which I dreamed.

One day I received a phone call from a recruiter. He was looking to fill a position in Florida for one of the largest and most prestigious ad agencies in the world, working on a mega-account. This particular agency was known for their forward thinking and cool culture. Here were the main points of his pitch:

- I would have a "virtual" office. The agency didn't have an office in the town where the job was located, so I could work from wherever I wanted. In fact, the recruiter encouraged me to work from the beach! My boss would be in New York, so I would have almost complete autonomy.
- I would be issued a state-of-the-art laptop computer, mobile phone, and whatever else I needed or wanted to set up shop. This was a big deal at the time because laptop computers were relatively new. I didn't know anyone who owned one. The same could be said for mobile phones. They were still the size of a brick. The only people who carried mobile phones at that time were people like the Gordon Gekko character from the 1987 movie *Wall Street*.
- I would receive a generous relocation package including assistance in finding a great home near the beach. A relocation specialist would ensure an easy transition. Everything would be taken care of.
- I would receive a substantial pay raise and signing bonus. In addition to that, Florida didn't have a state income tax, which meant that I would have more spending money to

enjoy my new life. And, of course, the company provided a comprehensive benefits package.

- Finally, the agency offered the prestige of an impressive brand name as did the client I would serve. It was the job I had always wanted.

The recruiter loved my qualifications and arranged interviews with a litany of people in New York with impressive sounding titles. His biggest concern was how quickly I could start. So, what do you think? Did I take the job?

Of course not. This story wouldn't be in this chapter if I had. In fact, I didn't even fly to New York for the interview process, which would have been a priceless experience for a twenty-something who aspired to work on Madison Avenue. I called the recruiter the minute I received my travel arrangements to turn down the opportunity. Here's how I justified my decision (reminder: this was a time before the internet and mobile devices were mainstream, so be gentle with your judgment):

- What in the world is a virtual office? I had to look up the word virtual to learn what it meant. This was a completely new concept. People work in offices. That's why we go to work, because work is somewhere else. The virtual office idea just seemed weird to me.

- He wants me to work from the beach? I would never get any work done.
- Won't it be lonely working all by myself?
- I have no clue how to use a laptop computer. Where would I plug it in at the beach? Who will show me how to use it? What if I get sand in the keyboard? Who will help me when the computer goes haywire?
- Ok, so admittedly the mobile phone sounded pretty cool. Although, I think we still called them car phones at that time. Where would I put it when I wasn't using it? Would I have to carry it around all the time? Would I have to slick my hair back like Gordon Gekko?
- What if I moved to Florida and the agency lost the account? I would surely lose my new job and find myself separated from the few business contacts I had back in Atlanta. I would be left stranded.
- Sure, it would be nice to earn more money, but I was doing fine. I had money for life's necessities and enough left over for a little fun.
- It would be nice to have impressive agency and client brand names on my resume, but how important is it really? I'll eventually find a job at one of the big agencies... right?

I found every possible reason to justify not taking the job. Making the move felt riskier than it actually was. Ironically, a few decades later I would write this book on a laptop computer, work in a virtual office (and yes, I have even worked on the beach), practically live on my mobile phone, find employment at a prestigious agency, win well-known global clients, lose well-known global clients, relocate to different parts of the country, move back to Atlanta, and ultimately make more money than I ever imagined back in my 20's. I eventually faced each of the frightening challenges on my list of justifications; somehow, I survived them all. In my mind at that time the risk out-weighed the reward, but my thinking was flawed. My aversion to risk was far greater than the actual risk. Things worked out for me in the end, but I sometimes wonder what else I've missed due to my aversion to risk?

A Bird in the Hand...

Why do we place a greater weight on risk than on reward, even when the odds are stacked in our favor?

One reason is *loss aversion*, which causes us to assign greater weight to potential negative out-comes than to potential positive outcomes. In terms of survival, this makes sense: if we have enough of what we need to survive, increasing our resources would be nice, but a decrease in our resources could be fatal. Because our brains are hard-wired to protect us from danger, situations we think of as risky cause an inordinate fear response. As a result, we tend to overestimate the odds of negative results, even when we may logically know better.

Let's consider three frightening events: a lightning strike, a plane crash, and a shark attack. These incidents rarely happen, but receive quite a bit of attention in the media when they do, serving to skew our sense of likelihood even further. These fears can become overpowering because they involve the greatest fear of all: death. But what are the odds?

According to National Geographic, "The odds of becoming a lightning victim in the U.S. in any one year is 1 in 700,000." The odds of dying in a plane crash are 1 in 11 million according to David Ropeik, a risk communication instructor at Harvard. MIT professor Arnold Barnett addressed our fear of flying in this way: "a traveler could on average fly once a day for 4 million years before succumbing to a fatal crash." And the odds of dying in a shark attack are 1 in 3.1 million. Even with these incredibly low odds, these fears are common enough to have been given names: aviophobia (fear of flying), galeophobia (fear of shark attack), and astraphobia (fear of lightning strike).

According to the National Safety Council if you really want something to worry about, the lifetime odds of dying in a motor vehicle accident is 1 in

103; unintentional poisoning is 1 in 119; and, dying from falling is 1 in 152. It turns out that everyday activities and hazards are statistically much more dangerous than headline grabbing (and rarely occurring) events, yet they don't produce the same level of fear or risk aversion.

Our perception of risk is usually distorted in favor of safety, but risk is only one side of the equation. The other side is reward. Consider the risk examples I gave earlier. The reward of flying may not be worth the perceived risk to someone with aviophobia. The reward of swimming in the ocean may not be worth the perceived risk for someone with galeophobia. And to be honest, I can't think of a reward for being out in a thunderstorm. Astraphobia is just plain common sense. However, one almost couldn't function in the modern world without participating in higher-risk activities like motor vehicle transportation, using the stairs, or taking prescribed medications (a common cause of poisoning). Risk perception and fear are driven by our emotional cognitive processing system, rather than rationality and analytics. That's why reasoning with someone in a fearful state seldom works. As Han Solo said, "Never tell me the odds." They rarely fit into our decision-making process anyway.

Remember Dr. Albrecht's five fear categories covered in the Momentary Lapse of Reason: Fear? Risk aversion plays on all five: Extinction,

Mutilation, Loss of Autonomy, Separation, and Ego Death. That's why risk aversion, the seventh deadly sin of decision making, is so powerful.

Obviously, I had no fear of mutilation or extinction as I considered the job in Florida. The reason we pass on business and career opportunities really has to do with the other three fears: Loss of autonomy, separation, and ego death.

In my mind, working on one enormous account was riskier than working on a portfolio of smaller accounts because if we lost the big account, I would most likely be out of a job. With the new job opportunity, I would have been a small cog on a much larger team; therefore, I would have had less power to affect my future. That is the fear of loss of autonomy. In my dream job scenario, I would have had to move to a different state and been separated from my friends and professional contacts. Remember, this was a time before social media, so connecting was more difficult. That is fear of separation.

I believe the main reason I chose not to pursue that job was fear of ego death. It was no secret to my family and friends that I wanted to work for a big-name agency. What if I landed my dream job and failed miserably at it? What if I weren't good enough? That was my greatest fear. My ego at the time couldn't take such a public embarrassment.

Always factor your natural loss aversion into any big decision; it may be keeping you from making the best choice.

Counting Cards

In the exploration of decision making and risk, there is probably no better arena to examine than gambling. Dictionary.com provides this definition for gambling (as a noun): "the act or practice of risking the loss of something important by taking a chance or acting recklessly." It offers this definition (as a verb): "to stake or risk money, or anything of value, on the outcome of something involving chance." And it defines chance as "the absence of any cause of events that can be predicted, understood, or controlled." Gambling sounds risky and unpredictable, so why would anyone ever do it?

As you probably know, lots of people do it. The American Gaming Association estimated the gross gaming revenue of regulated commercial casinos at $37.3 billion in 2012. Their definition of gross gaming revenue is "the amount wagered minus the winnings returned to players." That is just the tip of the iceberg. In 2015, NBA basketball commissioner Adam Silver raised eyebrows in a New York Times op-ed piece writing, "...some estimate that nearly $400 billion is illegally wagered on sports each year." Others estimate the number to be between $80 billion and $380 billion annually. The reality is we simply don't know because it is illegal and goes unreported. What we do know is billions and billions of dollars are spent on gambling every year.

So, why do so many people spend so much money gambling? Risk taking can be intoxicating. It's exciting. We get a natural high from it produced by a rush of adrenaline. Other factors include escapism, it is perceived as glamorous and it is a social activity. All of these reasons are associated with a heightened emotional state, not a rational, analytical mindset. Added to the emotional trigger is a misconception that many people have about gambling, that it is a low-risk, high-yield endeavor when, in fact, the opposite is true. This is not a recipe for sound decision making.

In his book, *Bringing Down the House: The Inside Story of Six MIT Students Who Took Vegas for Millions*, Ben Mezrich explains how a small group of college students made millions of dollars playing blackjack at casinos. During the week, they were normal college students; on the weekend, they were skilled card sharks gaming the gaming industry in Las Vegas. This story was made into a movie starring Kevin Spacey called *21*.

The technique they used to win big at the tables is called card counting. Although this practice is not illegal, it is frowned upon because it tips the scales of probability in favor of the player and away from the casino, or "house." When members of the MIT group were eventually identified, they were banned from the casinos. According to an article in the online edition of *The Tech*, an MIT student publication, "Eventually, members of the blackjack team were betrayed. Out of greed, some team members sold names and faces to the Griffin Agency, which is hired by some casinos to track players who win disproportionately. The Griffin Agency compiles a face book of card counters and prohibits them from betting.... [they get] the MIT freshman picture book every year."

What exactly is card counting and why do casinos hate this legal activity? It might be easiest to explain using the MIT group's favored game, blackjack. In this table game, each player is dealt two cards, and then must decide how many more cards to ask for. The goal is for your cards to total 21 without going over (for this reason, blackjack is also called Twenty-One). In a game like poker, the players compete against each other; in blackjack, it's the gambler versus the dealer. Blackjack has the best odds for the player, because the house only has a 1% edge. Even so, the dealer has the advantage: if the dealer gets a natural 21 with his first two cards, all other players automatically lose, except the players who also have cards totaling 21. They neither win nor lose. This is called "a push." The dealer is also bound by the rules of the house. For example, if his card value is lower than 17, he must take another card (called a hit). If his card value is seventeen or higher, he will not take another card, letting his hand stand.

The blackjack player has several decisions to make, but the two most basic and important are whether to take another card and how much to bet. On the surface, it may seem as if the outcome is influenced by luck, but like all games of chance, blackjack is a game of probabilities. The lavish Las Vegas hotels and casinos were built on the emotional decision making of most gamblers, but the MIT crew proved that mathematical strategies of probability are actually the key to the game. They understood that if they bet more money when the probabilities were in their favor and less money when they were in the dealer's favor, they would win money over time. In other words, this game of chance becomes less risky when you understand the probabilities.

The technique of counting cards focuses on the variable of which cards have already been dealt in order to determine the probabilities of which cards might be dealt next. For example, if you know that all the eights have been dealt, the probability of anyone at the table receiving another eight is zero. If you don't know how many eights have been dealt, you don't know the true probability of another eight coming from the dealer's deck. The card counter's advantage is in using this information to formulate more accurate probabilities to guide the player's decisions.

Contrary to popular belief, counting cards does not require the player to memorize the cards with *Rain Man* precision. The basic card counting strategy, called the Hi-Low method, requires the player to keep a "running count" of the cards that have been dealt. This is done by assigning each card a point value: low cards (1 through 6) = 1; neutral cards (7 through 9) = 0; high cards (10 through Ace) = -1. Let's say the following cards have been dealt: 2, 10, Ace, 6, 9, 7, 4, Queen, 2, 3, 8. The counter would translate those cards like this:

$1 + (-1) + (-1) + 1 + 0 + 0 + 1 + (-1) + 1 + 1 + 0$.

When all of these values are added, the total is two.

Again, the purpose of the Hi-Lo approach is to predict the ratio of high cards to low cards remaining in the deck. Statistically, when the deck has more high cards, it favors the player; low cards favor of the dealer. When the count is a positive number, bet more (the higher the count, the more you bet). When the count is negative, bet only the table minimum. In the example above, the player should bet more money.

Like everything else in life, it takes practice to master card counting. In addition to the skill itself, the player must learn to deal with the time pressure involved in a fast-moving game, the suspicious gaze of the pit boss, the all-seeing eye of casino security, waitresses, other players, and the myriad of buzzers, bells, and other distractions in a casino.

Successful card counting requires calm, rational decision making in the midst of chaos.

Why do most gamblers lose money? Because they make decisions based on emotion. They're riding a streak or making false assumptions based on the notion of luck. On the other hand, the MIT students were solving a math problem... over and over and over again. They didn't win every hand, but they played the probabilities to win more than they lost over a period of time. In fact, much more than they lost.

We all fall somewhere on the spectrum of risk tolerance. Some of us love to take risks, while others only go for sure things. Unfortunately, in the real world there are very few sure things. There is always the risk of failure. Depending on your risk tolerance, the perception of risk can be amplified too high or dimmed too low. The MIT students taught us that when emotion and fear are removed from a decision, risk is reduced to a metric of probability—a mere statistic, a calculated risk. And by using rational decision-making methods, we can win big.

Go For It!

What We Can Learn from The Coach Who Never Punts

Even when our decision making is at its most rational, others might not see it the same way. Trailblazing can be a lonely endeavor. One excellent example is Coach Kevin Kelley who challenged, but could not change, the accepted conventions of football.

In 2003, Kevin Kelley assumed the role of head football coach at Pulaski Academy in Little Rock, Arkansas. The football team had made it to the state semi-finals just twice in the 40 years prior to Kelley taking over. While he wanted to improve the team's performance, he knew two things: 1) the talent level of his players wouldn't dramatically increase; and, 2) there wouldn't be any rule changes forthcoming to provide them with a competitive advantage. Kelley understood that if his program continued to operate as it always had, their results would remain the same—mediocre. Therefore, he decided to look for ways to play the game differently to find a competitive edge. He examined every facet of the game and what he learned was groundbreaking.

At its core, football is a field-position game. Obviously, the objective is to score more points than your opponent, and the closer your team gets to the opponent's end zone, the higher your probability of scoring. Coaches have known this since 1869 when Rutgers played Princeton in what is widely considered the first college football game. Not only is it common sense, it is a fact supported by over a 145 years of statistics. It is this understanding that leads coaches to the convention of punting the ball to the opponent on fourth down.

To the uninitiated, this may seem counterintuitive: why give the ball away? The theory goes like this: we probably can't move the ball the distance we need to get a first down. So, rather than keeping the ball close to our end zone, we'll punt to get the ball as far away as possible and lower the opponent's probability of scoring.

Knowing the importance of field position in the game of football, would you consider it risky to stop punting altogether? Most coaches would. So when Coach Kelley adopted this strategy, to say it was unorthodox would be putting it mildly. When asked about his no-punt philosophy, the coach answered, "I don't think it's extremely risky." Let's look at the numbers.

When he took a deeper dive into the analytics of field position, Kelley learned that offenses score 77% of the time when they get within their opponents forty-yard line. The average net yardage gained from a high school punt is only 30 yards. Therefore, if Pulaski punted from deep in their own territory, the opponent would most likely receive the ball inside the forty-yard line, giving them a high probability of scoring. If punting means that the opponent scores most of the time, Kelley's rationale was, why do it?

Kelley's alternative was to "go for it" on fourth down, to keep driving forward rather than punting. This strategy gave the team an extra play to reach a first down and keep the offensive drive alive. Most teams punt when they are unable to gain ten yards in their first three downs. Because Pulaski doesn't punt, they have four downs to gain the same ten yards. Having four chances to achieve an objective is obviously better than having only three. That is Coach Kelley's competitive edge.

There are also advantages beyond the statistics. With an extra down, the offensive coordinator has the luxury of calling more aggressive plays in the first three downs. This makes Pulaski's play calling less predictable and more difficult for opponents to defend. Another advantage is that Pulaski players love this aggressive approach to the game. It is more fun and exciting; as any coach would attest, enthusiasm is an important driver of performance.

It doesn't stop there. While Kelley is known as the "coach who never punts," he is exploring additional unconventional tactics to provide his team with even more competitive advantages. For example, when he learned that teams with the fewest turnovers win over 80% of the time, he decided to force the issue. Pulaski uses onside kicks for every kickoff, giving them a better chance of recovering the ball, which Kelley considers a turn-over. Like his no-punt strategy, using onside kicks every time is unheard of in modern-day high school football. Yet, Pulaski Academy is successful at making the opponent turn over the ball on 20% of their kickoffs. That means they steal one out of every five kickoffs, which helps them to win the turnover battle.

Coach Kelley does things differently, but does his unorthodox style produce results? Yes, it does. Since Kevin Kelley became their head coach, the Pulaski Academy football team has won four state titles. As of December 2015, Pulaski had a 138-24-1 record, a remarkable .847 winning percentage. With such a track record of success, you would think everyone would adopt Coach Kelley's approach to the game.

As you've probably already guessed, you would be wrong. In an article for the *Citizen-Times (Asheville)*, reporter Keith Jarrett interviewed coaches from several of Pulaski Academy's opponents. Here is what some of them had to say about Kelley's strategies:

"I like my job, and I would like to keep it," said Coach Laws of Reynolds High. "If I did some of the things [Kelley is] doing, I don't think I would keep my job for very long."

"I've looked into that, but I just couldn't adhere to that kamikaze philosophy," said Coach Wilkins of Asheville High.

Coach Avery Cutshaw of Andrews said "I can see some of what he does having merit, but I'm a field-position coach, and that's what I believe in." At the time of that quote, Coach Cutshaw's football program was the least successful in the region, with a .243 winning percentage. What was Einstein's definition of insanity?

Coach Kelley's story has been known in football circles for years and yet coaches and "football insiders" around the country have not embraced his philosophy. With so much success, why hasn't Coach Kelley been hired to coach a college football team? So many college football programs are failing. Wouldn't it make sense to hire a proven winner with a system designed to level a playing field where disparities in talent typically determine win-loss records? And yet, as of the 2016 season, Kevin Kelley is still the coach of Pulaski Academy.

Coach Kelley's system was devised to reduce risk, create a competitive advantage, and produce more effective decision making in football games. His philosophy is based on hard analytics, and produces positive results. But history has shown that unorthodox ideas feel inherently risky.

Perceived risk has little to do with facts, statistics, or even results. Risk plays on our emotional thought processes, which are highly irrational. That's why coaches with losing records and losing programs find unconventional methods—no matter how successful—risky. "It all comes down to risk aversion," Kelley says. "The coaches I've talked to, a lot of them will say, 'We think you're right. We think we should.' But they're afraid of the media or the fans or losing their jobs. I think that's the bottom line." Coach Kelley gets it. Risks should be calculated, not based on irrational fear.

Vacc-a-phobia

The term conscientious objector did not originate in wartime. It was first used in English law to label parents who refused to vaccinate their children. These people risked both fines and imprisonment for their adamant opposition to the inoculation process of the only disease for which there was a human vaccine—smallpox.

In its time, smallpox killed millions. The mortality rate for adults with smallpox was 20% or more, while the mortality rate for children was over 30%. Smallpox was a vicious virus for survivors as well. In addition to the symptoms of fever and headache, smallpox sores often led to permanent scarring. In some cases, smallpox could even lead to blindness from corneal scarring.

In 1721, Lady Mary Wortley Montagu introduced Western society to a major breakthrough in the prevention of the spread of this deadly disease: inoculation. Using a method called arm-to-arm inoculation, fluid from a smallpox sore was introduced into a small cut in the skin of a healthy patient. The resulting infection would be less severe, and the mortality rate of those given the virus through inoculation was comparatively low: 1 in 200 versus 1 in 5. In 1798, Edward Jenner published his famous Inquiry introducing the concept of inoculating people with a safer animal virus called cowpox. The Latin word for cow, vacca, gave his inoculation process a new name—vaccination.

As with most scientific advancements, vaccination faced detractors. By 1889, well over one hundred anti-vaccination groups were protesting and publishing newsletters, even though 42,200 people had died in the smallpox epidemic of 1870–1872. Despite these protests, vaccination became more common and widespread, preventing countless deaths.

In 1967, smallpox was targeted for eradication around the world through the use of vaccination and surveillance-containment, a process of identifying and isolating patients infected with the virus. By 1980, the virus was officially declared eradicated by the World Health Organization. It was the first human disease eradicated with the use of vaccination.

Polio was another terrifying virus found around the globe. Outbreaks often occurred in the summer months, known as "polio season." While the disease was known as "infant paralysis," it also affected adults. The mortality rate of polio was much lower than that of smallpox, but polio could cause crippling paralysis in survivors.

1952 was an epidemic year for polio with 58,000 cases reported. Three thousand of those patients died and many more suffered varying degrees of lifelong paralysis. Hope finally arrived in March of 1953 when Dr. Jonas Salk, an American medical researcher at the University of Pittsburgh, announced that he had successfully developed a vaccine for the polio virus. After extensive testing, a nationwide vaccination campaign was implemented throughout the United States in 1955. By 1957, the number of new polio cases dropped to less than 6,000.

In 1962, Albert Sabin developed an oral version vaccine that greatly facilitated the distribution of the vaccine worldwide. While polio still exists in a few pockets around the world, it has been eliminated from the Western Hemisphere.

The inoculation process has been in use for hundreds of years, and is largely responsible for eradicating two of the most dangerous and terrifying diseases in the world. The process has saved countless lives and countless others have been spared the devastating effects of surviving these viruses, including scarring, blindness, and paralysis. And yet, a growing number of parents in the United States refuse to get their children vaccinated, primarily for three viruses that few of us have ever experienced: measles, mumps, and rubella.

Common symptoms for the measles virus include fever, runny nose, and conjunctivitis; the virus can cause pneumonia if it spreads to the lungs. Measles can also lead to encephalitis (inflammation of the brain) in older children, which can cause brain damage. According to the Centers for Disease Control and Prevention, roughly 1 in 1,000 measles patients will die as a result of the virus. Measles is highly contagious and is spread through droplets of spray released into the air when infected individuals cough or sneeze.

Prior to the widespread implementation of the measles vaccination in 1963, around three to four million people in the United States were infected each year, 48,000 were hospitalized, and between 400–500 died. Since the introduction of the vaccination, measles cases have declined by 99%; most cases today are imported by visitors from countries where measles is still common.

Patients with the mumps virus typically only experience swollen glands, but this virus was once the most common cause of acquired deafness and meningitis (inflammation of the lining of the brain and spinal cord). Like measles, this virus is spread through the air from coughing or sneezing. The mumps vaccine was introduced in 1967; as a result, cases of this virus have dropped by 99% in the United States.

Rubella, or German measles, is the least threatening of the three viruses for children, causing only a mild rash and swollen glands. However, if a pregnant woman contracts rubella in the first trimester, the impact on her baby could be traumatic. According to the Mayo Clinic: "Up to 90% of infants born to mothers who had rubella during the first 12 weeks of pregnancy develop Congenital Rubella Syndrome. This syndrome can cause one or more problems, including: growth retardation, cataracts, deafness, congenital heart defects, defects in other organs, mental retardation." In 1964–1965, prior to the development of the vaccine, an outbreak of rubella affected 12.5 million people. This outbreak resulted in around 20,000 cases of Congenital Rubella Syndrome in children: approximately 11,000 became deaf, 3,500 blind, and 1,800 had mental development issues. There were also 2,100 neonatal deaths as a result of this viral outbreak.

The first rubella vaccine was introduced in 1969. An improved version replaced it in 1979 and is still in use today. While rubella was declared eliminated in the United States in 2004, there is still a risk of the virus being imported by people from areas of the world where the virus is active.

Individually, the vaccines preventing measles, mumps, and rubella proved extremely effective, so in 1971 medical professionals began giving these vaccinations in a combination, commonly called the MMR vaccination. For nearly 45 years, these vaccinations have helped to alleviate pain, suffering, lifelong maladies, and death in the United States and around the world. The spread of these viruses is easily prevented. So why are parents refusing to get their children vaccinated?

One major cause of these parents' concern is an infamous study by Andrew Wakefield, et al., published in 1998 in the British journal, *The Lancet*. The study reported a causal connection between the MMR vaccine and autism spectrum disorder, or ASD.

ASD occurs in all ethnic and socioeconomic groups. Males are four times more likely to be diagnosed with the condition. Symptoms are often noticed between 12–18 months of age. As of the writing of this passage, scientists do not know what causes ASD, but it is believed that a combination of genetics and environmental factors are involved.

According to the National Institute of Neurological Disorders and Stroke, ASD "is a range of complex neurodevelopment disorders characterized by social impairments, communication difficulties, and restricted, repetitive, and stereotyped patterns of behavior." Symptoms vary greatly along the ASD spectrum, but individuals with ASD typically find it challenging to communicate with and relate to others. They may have an intense focus and preoccupation with specific objects or topics. They may also be inflexible with regard to routines and rituals. These factors make it difficult for people diagnosed with ASD to navigate the nuances of social interaction.

In the 1970's and 1980's around 1 in 2,000 children reportedly had autism. The CDC reports that diagnoses of ASD more than doubled between 2000 and 2010. In 2000, about 1 in 150 children were diagnosed; by 2010, 1 in 68 individuals reportedly had ASD. Those increases are alarming; to make matters worse, scientists cannot pinpoint a cause for the increase.

Because of the study published in *The Lancet*, many parents considered the MMR vaccine a possible trigger to ASD. After all, children begin to show signs of autism around the time they receive the vaccination, and while the scientific and medical communities insist these vaccinations are safe, they still cannot tell us what causes autism. A significant number of parents began to refuse vaccination, putting their own children and others at risk for contracting measles, mumps, and rubella.

As it turned out, the study that had gained so much traction with the public and struck fear into the hearts of new parents was a fake. An investigation by Brian Deer published through a series of articles in the *British Medical Journal* revealed that Mr. Wakefield had falsified records and data. *The Lancet* later retracted the study, and ten of its twelve authors removed their names from the work.

The medical community has worked hard to reverse the damage done to the perception of safety of the MMR vaccination. According to a statement on the American Academy of Pediatrics website, "Over the years, the Institute of Medicine and the AAP have organized several panels of independent scientists—all concluded that there is no association between MMR and autism."

And they had plenty of evidence before them. The dramatic rise in reported ASD incidence began over two decades after the introduction of the MMR vaccine, in the late 1990's and into the 2000's. If the vaccine were the culprit, there should have been an increase in ASD diagnoses in the mid-1970s.

In fact, the increase in ASD diagnoses might not indicate a rise in ASD cases at all. Decades ago, a child might have been given a generic "mentally challenged" label rather than being diagnosed with a specific condition such as ASD. With a better understanding of autism, and an expanded definition of the condition, doctors can now more accurately diagnose and help those children.

Surprisingly, most of those who hold onto the fear of vaccinations are well-educated, upper-middle and upper-class parents, people well able to access and understand the new evidence. Given what we know about risk perception, however, it is not surprising that statistics, odds, and probabilities would have little effect on such an emotionally charged decision.

If you are of primary child-bearing age, it is likely that you have never known anyone with a case of measles, mumps, or rubella (or, thankfully, smallpox or polio). These illnesses, once very real fears for parents, seem now to be only a historical footnote. However, the odds are pretty good that you have known someone on the ASD spectrum, or the parent of a child with ASD. If you don't know someone personally, you may have formed a relationship with someone on the internet. Anti-vaccination communities have a strong presence on social media, members sharing personal and "friend of a friend" stories, and supporting each other in their decision not to vaccinate.

Parents often trust the opinions of other parents over scientific data. Stories and anecdotes from friends and family carry more weight in our decision making than information from professionals like scientists and doctors. Dr. Kristin Hendrix, a professor at the Indiana University School of Medicine, explains: "Some folks are very predisposed to trust information about others' personal experience.... Even if the situation that a person hears about didn't actually happen to their friend or family member, but is being relayed by them, they trust that more than a face-to-face conversation with a physician." She continues, "That information, anecdote, narrative, personal account, rare instance that may or may not be true, tends to carry more gravity and weight when it comes from someone they know."

Parents may fear a negative reaction to a vaccine more than the actual disease it prevents because they have control over the decision to inoculate their child. In other words, if something goes wrong with the vaccination or if the child develops autism, the parent might feel some level of responsibility. Vaccinating the child was their decision after all. On the other hand, there is always the likelihood that an un-vaccinated child will not contract the measles, mumps, or rubella. If the child does get sick, the parent has effectively deflected responsibility for the illness as an act of nature. While they might have prevented the infection, they did not actually cause it. It wasn't their fault.

Risk perception is personal and emotional, and it plays on our most primal emotion: fear. A parent's decision about vaccination involves the health of our children, which most of us value over our own. We love them and we bear the responsibility for their safety. On a biological level, our offspring represent the survival of our genes here on earth. For these reasons, the perceived risk of vaccination, no matter how small, is elevated well beyond the reward of avoiding the MMR viruses. For many parents, facts, statistics and professional opinions are simply not enough to persuade them to vaccinate their children.

On the Flip Side of Risk Aversion

Fear is bundled into the risk equation and it distorts our perception of reality. Think of risk and reward as an equation with several variables. Our risk-averse nature tends to assign a higher value to the negative variables than they deserve and a lower weight to the positive variables. This distortion leads us to the conclusion that an opportunity is riskier than it really is. Did you notice I used the word "assign" in our weight distribution of negative variables? That is because our primitive emotional brain takes over the decision making in order to protect us from negative outcomes. Therefore, the weights we assign the negatives are often irrationally high.

Some people have a higher risk tolerance and they tend to undervalue the negative risk variables. Just know that we all have some semblance of risk aversion, it tends to turn up when the stakes are highest and it affects our decision making.

On the flip side, what if someone else's risk aversion (or lack thereof) has a negative impact on you? Remember, when someone is highly risk averse, their mind irrationally overweighs the negative variables, which skews the risk/reward ratio. Simply introducing a risk-averse person to more facts won't necessarily help them think rationally. That's because the emotional mind is making the risk assessment, not the rational mind. Therefore, we must focus on the emotional mind to influence a person in that state of mind. Here are a few strategies to avoid being the victim of a risk-averse decision maker:

Establish the decision maker's ownership in the right choice. This utilizes the *endowment effect*, where we value items that we possess more than items that we do not. Many of us find it difficult to get rid of things we don't need, because possession is tightly linked to control. When things feel out of control, we find things to possess because it makes us feel more in control. You might call this retail therapy.

My friend Emery loved to negotiate for automobiles. Believe it or not, he did it for fun. He once told me that car salesmen want you to take a car home for the night because it dramatically increases the likelihood that you will purchase it. This is the endowment effect at play in the real world. Emery would turn the tables on the salesman by returning the car to the dealership after keeping it for a night (or sometimes two or three) and not making an offer. At that point, the salesman felt like he was losing a sale he thought was a sure thing; given that most car salesmen work on commission, it could be said the salesman felt he "owned" that sale. To regain his lost commission, he was usually willing to cut a better deal.

The human response to diminishing personal control is called *psychological reactance*, which is the desire to preserve our established freedoms. Whenever free choice of goods or services is limited or threatened, we want them significantly more than before. This is why scarcity can drive demand. When an item is rare, or becoming rare, we find it more valuable.

Dr. Robert Cialdini says new scarcity is more powerful than constant scarcity. In other words, the drop from relative abundance to scarcity produces a greater reaction than constant scarcity. He writes, "We are most likely to find revolutions at a time when a period of improving economic and social conditions is followed by a short, sharp reversal in those conditions." Revolutionaries tend to be people who have been given some taste of the good life and then lose it.

How do you give someone "ownership" of an idea? Plant the seed, then walk away and let it grow in the decision maker's mind. When discussing the choices, provide all the benefits of the "right" idea and really make it shine. The key here is to avoid trying to sell the idea. Rather, plant it in the conversation and then let it go. It's best if the decision maker takes the idea and runs with it in that initial meeting. If not, mention the idea in a subsequent meeting: "I really liked that idea you had when we met last...." Most people will take ownership of the idea. Often, they will bring up the idea on their own after giving it time to germinate. They will assume it was their idea all along. Possession is $9/10^{th}$ of the law!

Give your decision maker a taste of the opportunity. Let them take the car home for the night. Make them feel as if they own the better choice. They won't want to let it go.

Redefine success. In other words, change the variables in the risk equation to make success appear to be less risky. Coach Kelley realized the team that wins the turnover battle typically wins the football game. So he implemented a strategy to force more turnovers. In essence, he redefined a successful onside kick as a turnover. Therefore, an 80% "failure" rate on onside kicks was acceptable to him because it increased his probability of winning the game. For Coach Kelley, the reward of successfully recovering one onside kick was worth the risk of giving up precious field position.

Perfectionists tend to be risk averse because they have a heightened fear of failure. They put themselves under tremendous pressure to succeed and will often avoid something that doesn't guarantee success. To overcome this fear, it helps to redefine the parameters of success for the decision maker. For Coach Kelley, a one-in-five success rate of recovering an onside-kick is a successful ratio; therefore, the four unsuccessful attempts are simply part of the greater success equation. Success is not defined by one failure but by the combined results of taking calculated risks.

Make it a "yes or no" decision. For the MIT card counters, the decision to bet big was a yes or no choice based on simple math. If my running count is X, I bet big; if my running count is negative X, I bet small. The emotion of gambling and risk aversion was taken out of the equation (for the most part). The decision was made easy.

While you can't take the emotion out of decision making entirely, you can help a decision maker focus on one important variable. Frame it as a yes or no decision based on that variable. The challenge is that their irrational mind won't always want to focus on the right variable. It is up to you to steer them in the right direction.

Entice the decision maker to lust for the opportunity. For the most part, you can't influence a risk-averse decision maker unless you induce emotional arousal. We are more easily influenced when we desire something, so raise the emotional stakes whenever possible.

Jobs at big-name ad agencies were hard to come by in the early 1990's, and that big-agency position really was my dream job. If I could go back, older me would leverage that emotion to stoke the fire in the younger me. I should have been willing to do anything to get that job, but my emotional arousal (or desire) wasn't strong enough to overcome my risk aversion.

Provide a safety net. When failure is an option, here's the plan B. The goal of providing a safety net is to reduce the perceived risk that keeps the decision maker from making the better choice. It's a "get out of jail free" card. If there is no downside, there is really no risk for the decision maker. Discuss what the decision maker might do if the chosen option doesn't work out. Beware: sometimes just knowing that there is a plan B will lure the fearful, risk-averse decision maker to employ it before they have fully exhausted plan A. Be strategic with your plan B option: its only purpose is to minimize the perceived risk of the best option to enable the decision maker to really go for it. Make option A the obvious best choice, and get them to declare it publicly. That will establish ownership in the decision.

Our brain's main job is to ensure survival. It hates risk—even when taking a calculated risk can lead to great rewards. Sometimes it's necessary to override our internal processing system to make better decisions.

CONCLUSION

By now you have probably noticed the common thread in each of the seven deadly sins of decision making—the unconscious mind. The sins are more likely to occur when our cognitive processing has switched to autopilot. Our minds typically run on both analytical and autopilot cognitive systems simultaneously, although one system tends to be in control... usually it's autopilot. Even when we are in a rational, controlled, conscious state of mind, one of the momentary lapses of reason may activate autopilot thinking. While it is impossible to engage our analytical processing system all of the time, we can learn to activate it in important, high-stakes situations. This is a cognitive skill like any other, and it takes practice. The key to combatting auto-pilot decisions is *awareness*.

First, recognize the momentary lapses of reason that trigger autopilot thinking: too little information, too much information, time pressure, emotional arousal, and fear. For example, if I recognize that I don't have enough information to make a particular decision, I know that I am susceptible to stereotyping, false attribution, and being overly attracted to the familiar. That awareness can keep me from falling prey to autopilot thinking and the poor decisions that may result.

Second, question your assumptions. Why do I assume this person is knowledgeable or unknowledgeable about this topic? Why am I gravitating toward this idea, person, or object? Have I made an assumption about their competence or personality based on a particular characteristic? Do they or do they not look the part? Am I simply choosing someone or something that I have chosen before? Learning where your blind spots are can help you avoid costly mistakes.

On the flip side, we can use that same awareness to influence the decision making of others. I encourage you to continue your studies in the field of influence beginning with the references listed in the *Notes and References* section of this book. As you practice awareness of the seven deadly sins of decision making, you will find them easier to recognize in others than in yourself. That is because the decision maker is operating on autopilot, but you are thinking clearly. Your influence in those moments can be very powerful. Use it wisely.

I began researching this material in earnest because of an experience with an executive who was making a terrible decision that would negatively affect his business and his employees. I could plainly see the mistake and tried to convince him to choose another path. He wouldn't listen to reason. The results were disastrous and I blamed myself. At the time, I didn't have the tools to influence his decision making. I have them now—and so do you.

Go make good decisions.

NOTES & REFERENCES

Introduction

The quote was taken from an article written by Ni, Preston. "8 Negative Attitudes of Chronically Unhappy People." *Psychology Today*. 22 Feb. 2015. Web.

Chapter 2

Many of the psychological terms were defined using this textbook: Braisby, Nick and Angus Gellatly. *Cognitive Psychology*. 2nd ed. Oxford, England: Oxford, 2012. Print. 694. They were also vetted by psychology professors Dr. Jeannine Jannot and Dr. Frank Provenzano.

The definition of "bias" was taken from Dictionary.com Unabridged. Random House, Inc. 16 Jul. 2015.<Dictionary.com http://dictionary.reference.com/browse/bias>. Web.

The definition for "fallacy" was taken from Daniel Kahneman's *Thinking, Fast and Slow*. New York: Farrar, Straus and Giroux, 2011. Print. 158. This is such a thorough and informative book about how we think and the things that affect our decision making. Dr. Kahneman won the Nobel Prize in Economics.

When the Emotional Tail Wags the Rational Dog
The Carl Jung quote comes from Peter Murray's article, "Carl Jung...Consumer Psychologist?" *Psychology Today.* 12 Mar. 2014. Web.
https://www.psychologytoday.com/blog/inside-the-consumer-mind/201403/carl-jungconsumer-psychologist

David Ropeik summed up our cognitive operating systems nicely in the following articles:
"Think You Are in Charge of Your Thinking? Think Again!" *Psychology Today.* 29 May 2014. Web.
https://www.psychologytoday.com/blog/how-risky-is-it-really/201405/think-you-are-in-charge-your-thinking-think-again

Ropeik, David. "Are These Dangerous Times, or Do They Just Feel That Way?" *Psychology Today.* 2 Jan. 2015 Web.
https://www.psychologytoday.com/blog/how-risky-is-it-really/201501/are-these-dangerous-times-or-do-they-just-feel-way

I used the terms *analytical* and *autopilot* to define the two human operating systems, rather than the terms used by Dr. Ropeik and Dr. Kahneman: System 1 and System 2.

Chapter 3

The Magic Word: "Because"
Many people have written about the power of "because" and the Copy Machine Study. The following resources were my main references for this section:

Weinschenk, Susan and Wise, Brian. "The Power of the Word "Because" To Get People To Do Stuff." *Psychology Today*. 15 Oct. 2013 Web.

https://www.psychologytoday.com/blog/brain-wise/201310/the-power-the-word-because-get-people-do-stuff

Dobelli, Rolf. *The Art of Thinking Clearly*. New York, NY. 2013. HarperCollins. Pp. 155–157.

Clear, James. "The One Word That Drives Senseless and Irrational Habits." *Jamesclear.com*. Web.

http://jamesclear.com/copy-machine-study

Because I'm A Good Father
Peter Noel Murray sums up my motivations for buying those two cars in his article, "Why We Really Shop." *Psychology Today*. 11 Jun. 2014. Web.
https://www.psychologytoday.com/blog/inside-the-consumer-mind/201406/why-we-really-shop. More on this in the *On the Flip Side* of this chapter.

Dr. Murray provides additional rationale in this article: "I Am My Ferrari." *Psychology Today*. 6 Oct. 2011. Web.
https://www.psychologytoday.com/blog/inside-the-consumer-mind/201110/i-am-my-ferrari. At least I didn't buy a Ferrari!

The Best and Brightest
Information about the MIT Sloane School of Management came from their website: "About MIT Sloane." 20 Mar. 2015. Web. http://mitsloan.mit.edu/about-mit-sloan/

Gary Kline's book on decision making is a must read for influencers. It is one of the seminal works in this field: *Sources of Power, How People Make Decisions*. Cambridge: The MIT Press, 1998. Print. 10–11. The Soelberg story referenced in *The Siren's Call* is from this book.

Going For Broke
The economic data about the great recession came from these three sources:

U.S. Bureau of Labor and Statistics. *The Recession of 2007–2009*. Feb. 2012. Web.
http://www.bls.gov/spotlight/2012/recession/

The Conference Board.
https://www.conference-board.org/data/consumerconfidence.cfm

U.S. Bureau of Economic Analysis. *Personal Savings Rate*. 2 Mar. 2015. Web.
https://research.stlouisfed.org/fred2/data/PSAVERT:txt

Berman, Jillian. "75 Percent of Americans Don't Have Enough Savings to Cover Their Bills For Six Months: Survey." *Huffington Post*. 24 Jun. 2013. Web.
http://www.huffingtonpost.com/2013/06/24/americans-savings_n_3478932.html

Chuck Jaffe's article did a wonderful job of listing the justifications we make to avoid saving for retirement: "5 Lies People Tell Themselves about Saving for Retirement." *Market Watch*. 22 Feb. 2015. Web.
http://www.marketwatch.com/story/5-lies-people-tell-them-selves-about-saving-for-retirement-2015-02-20

Professional player salaries came from Kurt Badenhausen's article: "Average MLB Player Salary Nearly Double NFL's, But Still Trails NBA's." *Forbes*. 23 Jan. 2015. Web.
http://www.forbes.com/sites/kurtbadenhausen/2015/01/23/average-mlb-salary-nearly-double-nfls-but-trails-nba-play-ers/#71f98bd9269e

The reasons pro athletes go broke came from Russ Wiles article: "Pro Athletes Often Fumble the Financial Ball." *USA Today*. 22 Apr. 2012.
http://usatoday30.usatoday.com/sports/story/2012-04-22/Pro-athletes-and-financial-trouble/54465664/1

James Marshall Crotty's quote and the financial information about Allen Iverson came from his article in Forbes: "Allen Iverson Earned Over $200 Million in His NBA Career. Now He's Reportedly Broke. Say, What?" *Forbes*. 21 Feb. 2012. Web. http://www.forbes.com/sites/jamesmarshallcrotty/2012/02/21/allen-iverson-earned-over-200-million-in-his-nba-career-hes-now-broke-say-what/

Jones Envy

Albert Walker provides a thorough history of the Jones family on this website: "Keeping Up with the Joneses." 2009. Web. http://www.jonesnyhistory.com

William Safire wrote about social mobility and keeping up with the Jonses in this article: "On Language: Up the Down Ladder." 15 Nov. 1998. *The New York Times Magazine*. Web. http://www.nytimes.com/1998/11/15/magazine/on-language-up-the-down-ladder.html?src=pm

Members Only jackets have apparently made a comeback. You can purchase your very own Members Only jacket here: http://www.membersonlyoriginal.com

The Power of Authority

This quote came from Paco Underhill's enlightening book *Why We Buy, The Science of Shopping*. Updated and Revised. New York: Simon & Shuster, 1999. Print.

On The Flip Side Of Justifying
Douglas Van Praet's article covers many of the concepts in this chapter. I encourage you to read it: "7 Unconscious Errors We Make When Buying Brands, Our Purchase Decisions Can Be Highly Irrational and Costly." *Psychology Today*. 12 Jan. 2014. https://www.psychologytoday.com/blog/unconscious-branding/201401/7-unconscious-errors-we-make-when-buying-brands

As I mentioned earlier, my motivations for purchasing those two Mercedes were summed up nicely by Peter Noel Murray in these two articles: "Why We Really Shop." *Psychology Today*. 11 Jun. 2014. Web. https://www.psychologytoday.com/blog/inside-the-consumer-mind/201406/why-we-really-shop

Murray, Peter Noel. "I Am My Ferrari." *Psychology Today*. 6 Oct. 2011. Web. https://www.psychologytoday.com/blog/inside-the-consumer-mind/201110/i-am-my-ferrari

I would like to thank Dr. Robert Cialdini for piquing my interest in the science of influence with his book *Influence, Science, and Practice*. 5th ed. Boston: Pearson Education Inc., 2009. Print. Reading this book was opening Pandora's box for me. Much of the information on consistency and authority was sourced from this book.

The tactic of setting expectations came from Dan Ariely's *Predictably Irrational, The Hidden Forces That Shape Our*

Decisions. Revised and Expanded Edition. New York: HarperCollins, 2009. Print. 160. This is another of my favorite books on decision making and influence. It is a must-read for anyone wishing to learn more about this topic.

These were my sources for the power of *because*:
Weinschenk, Susan and Wise, Brian. "The Power of The Word 'Because' To Get People To Do Stuff." *Psychology Today.* 15 Oct. 2013 Web.
https://www.psychologytoday.com/blog/brain-wise/201310/the-power-the-word-because-get-people-do-stuff

Dobelli, Rolf. *The Art of Thinking Clearly.* New York, NY. 2013. HarperCollins. Pp. 155–157.

The concept of suggested memories came from Paco Underhill's book *Why We Buy, The Science of Shopping.* Updated and Revised. New York: Simon & Shuster, 1999. Print.

Chapter 4

The Dr. Fox Effect
Information on the Dr. Fox Effect came from these two sources:

Vitelli, Romeo. "The Return of Dr. Fox." *Psychology Today.* 5 May, 2014. Web.
https://www.psychologytoday.com/blog/media-spot-light/201405/the-return-dr-fox

Naftulin, Donald H., John E. Ware, Jr., and Frank A. Donnelly. "The Doctor Fox Lecture: A Paradigm of Educational Seduction." *Journal of Medical Education*, vol. 48, July 1973, p. 630–635. Web.
http://www.er.uqam.ca/nobel/r30034/PSY4180/Pages/Naftulin.html

As of this writing, the actual video of the Dr. Fox lecture is posted on YouTube.

The power of the appearance of authority came from Dr. Cialdini's *Influence, Science and Practice*. 5th ed. Boston: Pearson Education Inc., 2009. Print.

What Does Strength Look Like?

I read *The Rogue Warrior* over a decade before I read anything about the science of influence. Marcinko's passage about stereotyping really stuck with me. My father grew up on Key West, FL and saw SEAL Team training methods up close and personal. I heard stories about them from a very young age and hold all of the U.S. Special Forces in high regard. When I began writing this book, I knew that I had to include a section about the special forces and Marcinko's quote. Here is the official source reference:

Marcinko, Richard and John Weisman. *The Rogue Warrior*. New York: Pocket Books, 1992. Print. 49-50.

I would like to thank Malcolm Gladwell for inspiring me to write about the topic of decision making. After reading *The*

Tipping Point and *Blink*, I challenged myself to present this material using stories and articles, rather than a textbook writing style. It was much more fun to write and I hope you found it more interesting to read. I first read the term *thin-slicing* in Malcolm Gladwell's *Blink: The Power of Thinking Without Thinking*. New York: Little, Brown, 2005. Print. 23.

What Does an American Look Like?
Benjamin Franklin was an absolutely fascinating man. Information used for this passage came from Walter Isaacson's wonderful book, *Benjamin Franklin, An American Life*. New York: Simon & Schuster Paperbacks, 2003. Print. 38, 54, 328. I encourage you to pick up a copy.

On The Flip Side Of Stereotyping
Stereotype. *Merriam-Webster Dictionary*. Web.
http://www.merriam-webster.com/dictionary/stereotype

Dr. Robert Cialdini explains stereotyping as a cognitive simplification process in *Influence, Science, and Practice*. 5th ed. Boston: Pearson Education Inc., 2009. Print. 7–8, 146-148. I also found the higher pay for attractive people statistic in this book.

The Burger King study came from Dr. Nancy Etcoff's book *Survival of the Prettiest: The Science of Beauty*. New York: Random House, 1999. Print. This is an engrossing book about the science behind "lookism." I also got the data about the height of Fortune 500 CEOs from this book, page 173.

The percentage of adult men six feet tall or taller came from Malcolm Gladwell's *Blink: The Power of Thinking Without Thinking*. New York: Little, Brown, 2005. Print. 87.

The information in the passage on President Obama's suit came from Eric Dodds' article "In Defense of Barack Obama's Tan Suit." *Time*. 29 Aug. 2014. Web.
http://time.com/3214633/barack-obama-tan-suit/

This is my favorite book on body language: Pease, Allan and Barbara Pease. *The Definitive Book of Body Language*. New York: Bantam Dell, 2004. Print. I have been recommending it for years, especially for people who are actively interviewing.

Proverbs 13:20. *King James Version Gift & Award Bible*. Revised. Grand Rapids: Zondervan, 2002. Print.

Robert Greene's book is the most comprehensive book on power that I have read: *The 48 Laws of Power*. New York: Penguin Books, 1998. Print. I have given copies to a number of high-level executive colleagues.

Chapter 5

"Correlation." Merriam-Webster, Incorporated. 2016. Web.
http://www.merriam-webster.com/dictionary/correlation

"Causation." Dictionary.com Unabridged. Random House, Inc. 7 Nov. 2016. Web.
http://www.dictionary.com/browse/causation?s=t

The *conjunction fallacy* definition is from this textbook: Braisby, Nick and Angus Gellatly. *Cognitive Psychology*. 2nd ed. New York: Oxford. 2012. Print. 335.

"Placebo Effect: What Is It?" WebMD, LLC. 2016. Web. http://www.webmd.com/pain-management/what-is-the-placebo-effect

Tyler Vigen's website is fascinating. He has updated his "Spurious Correlations" since the time I first wrote this piece. Check back often. It is worth your time. Spurious Media, LLC. 2016. Web.
http://www.tylervigen.com/spurious-correlations

The Asian (Dis)Advantage
All of the census information came from the United States Census, 2010. Web.
http://www.census.gov.

Information on the Asian immigration timetable and circumstances came from www.asian-nation.org.

Information about Asian admission standards came from Frank Shyong's article "For Asian Americans, a Changing Landscape on College Admissions." *Los Angeles Times*. 21 Feb. 2015. Web.
http://www.latimes.com/local/california/la-me-adv-asian-race-tutoring-20150222-story.html#page=1

Ellen Rosen wrote about complaints filed against Harvard in this article: "Asian-American Group Says Harvard Discriminates." *Bloomberg Business*. 18 May 2015. Web.
http://www.bloomberg.com/news/articles/2015-05-18/asian-american-group-says-harvard-discriminates-business-of-law

Melvin Backman's quote came from his article, "Asian-American Families are Closing the Racial Wealth Gap the Fastest." *Quartz*. 27 Feb. 2015. Web.
http://qz.com/352059/asian-american-families-are-closing-the-racial-wealth-gap-the-fastest/

Atari's Pitfall

The information about Atari and the video game industry crash of 1983 came from these three sources:

Oxford, Nadia. "Ten Facts about the Great Video Game Crash of '83" *IGN*. 21 Sep. 2011. Web.
http://www.ign.com/articles/2011/09/21/ten-facts-about-the-great-video-game-crash-of-83

Buchanan, Levi. "Top 10 Best-Selling Atari 2600 Games." *IGN*. 26 Aug. 2008. Web.
http://www.ign.com/articles/2008/08/26/top-10-best-selling-atari-2600-games

Llorca. Juan Carlos. "Diggers Find Atari's E.T. Games In Landfill". *Associated Press*. 26 Apr. 2014. Web.
http://bigstory.ap.org/article/diggers-ready-unearth-ataris-et-games-0

The information about the economic downturn in 1983 came from the U.S. Bureau of Labor Statistics. http://www.bls.gov

Why Men Are Smarter Than Women
The IQ information came from Satoshi Kanazawa's article "Why Are Men More Intelligent Than Women." *Psychology Today.* 18 Jan. 2009. Web.
https://www.psychologytoday.com/blog/the-scientific-fundamentalist/200901/why-men-are-more-intelligent-women

The height of the U.S. Presidents came from www.presidenstory.com, 20 Mar. 2015. Web.

Average height for men came from *FastStats.* Centers for Disease Control and Prevention. Web.
http://www.cdc.gov/nchs/fastats/body-measurements.htm

Carl Jung's take on complexes came from Elaine Aron's article "Watch Out for Those Touchy, Treacherous, Hurting Complexes." *Psychology Today.* 22 Feb. 2011. Web.
https://www.psychologytoday.com/blog/attending-the-undervalued-self/201102/watch-out-those-touchy-treacheroushurting-complexes

Information on the Napoleon Complex came from Mark Van Vugt's article "Napoleon Complex in Football: The Beautiful Game Turned Ugly." *Psychology Today.* 7 Jun. 2011. Web.
https://www.psychologytoday.com/blog/naturally-selected/201106/napoleon-complex-in-football-the-beautifulgame-turned-ugly

Nancy Etcoff mentions the correlation between size and dominance in the animal kingdom in, *Survival of the Prettiest: The Science of Beauty*. New York: Random House, 1999. Print. 172-173, 176.

Information on the establishment of hierarchy came from Jeff Wise's article, "Who'll Be the Alpha Male? Ask the Hormones." *Psychology Today*. 4 Oct. 2010. Web. https://www.psychologytoday.com/blog/extreme-fear/201010/wholl-be-the-alpha-male-ask-the-hormones

The fact that tall men have higher self-esteem came from Susan Krauss Whitbourne's article, "Why Women Want Tall Men." *Psychology Today*. 15 Jun. 2013. Web. https://www.psychologytoday.com/blog/fulfillment-any-age/201306/why-women-want-tall-men

The height and income correlation reference came from Gad Saad's article "How Likely is a Woman to be Taller Than Her Man?" *Psychology Today*. 30 Jan. 2010. Web. https://www.psychologytoday.com/blog/homo-consumeri-cus/201001/how-likely-is-woman-be-taller-her-man. This article also provided the statistic on the percentage of couples where the woman is taller than the man.

The *tall man syndrome* concept came from this Susan Heitler article: "Success Can Breed the Narcissism of 'Tall Man Syndrome.'" *Psychology Today.* 27 Oct. 2011.
https://www.psychologytoday.com/blog/resolution-not-conflict/201110/success-can-breed-the-narcissism-tall-man-syndrome

Amy Wilson gave us the theory on why women are attracted to tall men in her article: "Tall Men Do Get The Girl." Relationships. *Psychology Today.* 1 May 2000. Web.
https://www.psychologytoday.com/articles/200005/relationships

Seth Meyers' quote came from this article: "Short Men: Why Women Aren't Attracted Enough to Date Them." *Psychology Today.* 3 Jan. 2014. Web.
https://www.psychologytoday.com/blog/insight-is-2020/201401/short-men-why-women-arent-attracted-enough-date-them

The Problem With Pedigree
Information on the number of Ivy League graduates on the Forbes 100 Most Powerful Women list, and the ROI of an Ivy League education came from Moira Forbes' article, "Does a Diploma from an Ivy League School Still Matter?" *Forbes.* 15 Aug. 2013. Web.
http://www.forbes.com/sites/moiraforbes/2013/08/15/does-an-ivy-league-diploma-still-matter/

The PayScale.com study information came from Kim Clark's article, "Graduates of these Colleges Make the Most Money (and It's Not Just the Ivies)." *Time.* 5 Mar. 2015. Web.
http://time.com/money/3732797/best-colleges-high-earnings/

The SAT score correlation with earnings came from Lynn O'Shaughnessy's article, "The Ivy League Earnings Myth." *U.S. News & World Report.* 1 Mar. 2011. Web.
http://www.usnews.com/education/blogs/the-college-solution/2011/03/01/the-ivy-league-earnings-myth

Ivy League college acceptance rates came from Janet Lorin's "Harvard, Stanford Reject 95 Percent of Applicants this Year." *Bloomberg Business.* 31 Mar. 2015. Web.
http://www.bloomberg.com/news/articles/2015-03-31/spurned-ivy-league-hopefuls-have-lots-of-company-in-their-misery

On the Flip Side of False Cause
The *self-fulfilling prophesy* definition came from Carolyn Kaufman's article "Using Self-Fulfilling Prophecies to Your Advantage." *Psychology Today.* 11 Oct. 2012. Web.
https://www.psychologytoday.com/blog/psychology-writers/201210/using-self-fulfilling-prophecies-your-advantage

Riggio, Ronald. "The 5 Psychological Traps We All Fall Into." *Psychology Today.* 26 Oct. 2014. Web.
https://www.psychologytoday.com/blog/cutting-edge-leadership/201410/the-5-psychological-traps-we-all-fall

The information on *self-serving attribution bias* came from Alice Boyes' article, "The Self-Serving Bias—Definition, Research, and Antidotes." *Psychology Today.* 9 Jan. 2013. Web.
https://www.psychologytoday.com/blog/in-practice/201301/the-self-serving-bias-definition-research-and-antidotes

Just-world phenomenon definition came from Travis Langley's article, "Spectacular Tragedy in a Just World: The Power of Why?" *Psychology Today.* 18 Apr. 2013. Web.
https://www.psychologytoday.com/blog/beyond-heroes-and-villains/201304/spectacular-tragedy-in-just-world-the-power-why

Victim mentality concepts come from Preston Ni's article, "8 Negative Attitudes of Chronically Unhappy People." *Psychology Today.* 22 Feb. 2015. Web.
https://www.psychologytoday.com/blog/communication-success/201502/8-negative-attitudes-chronically-unhappy-people

Momentary Lapse of Reason: Too Much Information
Information about cognitive overload triggering autopilot thinking came from Alain Samson's "On 'Cognitive Business': Observations on Being Cognitively Busy in Life and the Lab." *Psychology Today.* 22 Feb. 2012. Web.
https://www.psychologytoday.com/blog/consumed/201202/cognitive-business

Chapter 6

The Right Mix
Nancy Etcoff's quote came from her book, *Survival of the Prettiest: The Science of Beauty*. New York: Random House, 1999. Print. 39.

Buzzword Bingo
Gladwell, Malcolm. *The Tipping Point: How Little Things Can Make a Big Difference*. New York: Black Bay Books/Little, Brown and Company, 2000. Print.

Alain Samson's quote came from his article, "Seven Reasons Why We're Irrational Shoppers" *Psychology Today*. 25 Sep. 2013. Web.
https://www.psychologytoday.com/blog/consumed/201309/seven-reasons-why-were-irrational-shoppers

The Incumbent Advantage
Senator Coburn's quote and the election statistics came from Todd Phillips' article, "How Was 91 Percent of Congress Re-Elected Despite a 10 Percent Approval Rating?" *Huffington Post*. 13 Nov. 2012. Web.
http://www.huffingtonpost.com/todd-phillips/congress-election-results_b_2114947.html

Paul Steinhauser and Robert Yoon's quote came from their article, "Cost to Win Congressional Election Skyrockets." *CNN*. 11 Jul. 2013. Web.
http://www.cnn.com/2013/07/11/politics/congress-election-costs/

The congressional approval information and the percentage of citizens who know their House representative came from Chris Cillizza's article, "People Hate Congress. But Most Incumbents Get Re-Elected. What Gives?" *The Washington Post.* 9 May 2013. Web.
http://www.washingtonpost.com/blogs/the-fix/wp/2013/05/09/people-hate-congress-but-most-incumbents-get-re-elected-what-gives/

Why Brands Make Us Feel Better
The University of Cincinnati study information came from Beth Levine's article, "The Truth About Generics Vs. Brand-Name Medications." *The Huffington Post.* 22 Feb. 2015. Web.
http://www.huffingtonpost.com/2015/02/22/generic-prescriptions_n_6730194.html

On the Flip Side of Familiarity
Information about our preference for the familiar and the *mere exposure effect* came from Douglas Van Praet's article, "7 Unconscious Errors We Make When Buying Brands, Our Purchase Decisions Can Be Highly Irrational and Costly." *Psychology Today.* 12 Jan. 2014.
https://www.psychologytoday.com/blog/unconscious-branding/201401/7-unconscious-errors-we-make-when-buying-brands. This article also included Dr. Kahneman's concept and quote about what you see is all there is.

The information about the O.J. Simpson trial came from the powerful documentary, *O.J.: Made in America*, directed by Ezra Edelman. This five-part series was released in 2016 as a part of the ESPN 30 for 30 documentary series. It won an Academy Award for Best Documentary Feature among other awards. What made this documentary exceptional was the filmmakers' ability to provide context to the situation through a holistic perspective. I found it absolutely fascinating and I highly recommend it.

The notion that inconsistency is considered negative came from Robert Cialdini's book, *Influence, Science and Practice.* 5th ed. Boston: Pearson Education Inc., 2009. Print. 53 – 54, 129. The social proof reference came from this book as well.

The concept of believing memories to be factual accounts comes from Leonard Mlodinow's article, "The Illusion of Memory." *Psychology Today.* 15 May 2012. Web. https://www.psychologytoday.com/blog/subliminal/201205/the-illusions-memory

Neal Roese and Kathleen Vohs' quote came from their article, "We Never Saw It Coming." *Psychology Today.* 26 Nov. 2012. Web. https://www.psychologytoday.com/blog/in-hind-sight/201211/we-never-saw-it-coming

Chapter 7

The Sinking Lineup

Most of the baseball statistics and references came from www.baseball-reference.com, 2015. Web. The rest came from my extremely biased mind as a longtime Atlanta Braves fanatic. The news wasn't all bad for Frank Wren. After the Braves released him, Wren was hired by the Boston Red Sox as Senior Vice President of Baseball Operations in 2015. I hope he avoids the dreaded double down in his new position.

Ponzi's Pyramid

Information about Ponzi's life came from Mitchell Zuckoff's book *Ponzi's Scheme*. New York: Random House Trade Paperbacks, 2006. Print. I stumbled on this book while researching Bernie Madoff. I was originally going to write a section about Madoff, but Ponzi's story was so much more interesting I decided to write about him. I only covered a fraction of Ponzi's interesting life, so I highly recommend you pick up a copy of *Ponzi's Scheme* to learn more about this fascinating figure.

Flight Of The Concorde

I was always fascinated by the Concorde and knew people who flew on the impressive aircraft. By all accounts, it was every bit as luxurious and glamorous as its reputation. Information about the Concorde's specs and ticket prices came from Michael Gebicki's article "Everyone Asks: What Happened to the Concorde?" *Traveler*. 14 Jun. 2014. Web.
http://www.traveller.com.au/everyone-asks-what-happened-to-the-concorde-39wlc

Additional information came from Richard Westcott's article "Could Concorde Ever Fly Again? No, Says British Airways." *BBC News*. 24 Oct. 2013. Web.
http://www.bbc.com/news/business-24629451

On The Flip Side Of Doubling Down
The *ego death* reference came from Dr. Karl Albrecht's article "The Only 5 Fears We All Share." *Psychology Today.* 22 Mar. 2012. Web.
https://www.psychologytoday.com/blog/brainsnacks/201203/the-only-5-fears-we-all-share

The concept of emotional thinking over analytical thinking came from David Ropeik's article "Are These Dangerous Times, or Do They Just Feel That Way?" *Psychology Today.* 2 Jan. 2015. Web.
https://www.psychologytoday.com/blog/how-risky-is-it-really/201501/are-these-dangerous-times-or-do-they-just-feel-way

Momentary Lapse Of Reason: Emotional Arousal
The concept that consumers use emotions rather than analysis came from Peter Noel Murray's article. It also provided the fMRI information. "How Emotions Influence What We Buy." *Psychology Today.* 26 Feb. 2013. Web.
https://www.psychologytoday.com/blog/inside-the-consumer-mind/201302/how-emotions-influence-what-we-buy

The concept that we are more apt to satisfy our immediate desires when in an emotional state came from Alain Samson's article "Seven Reasons Why We're Irrational Shoppers." *Psychology Today*. 25 Sep. 2013. Web.

https://www.psychologytoday.com/blog/consumed/201309/ seven-reasons-why-were-irrational-shoppers. Also, the idea that compulsive shopping can affect the mood of someone with depression or sadness came from this article.

Chapter 8

If The Panties Fit

Paco Underhill's quote came from: *Why We Buy, The Science of Shopping*. Updated and Revised. New York: Simon & Shuster, 1999. Print. 214, 217.

Do They Know It's Christmas?

Spin Magazine was extremely brave in reporting the realities of the Live Aid story in 1986. They took a great deal of heat at the time from other media organizations, but the information in their story was eventually corroborated by legitimate news publications. Most of the information on the Live Aid situation came from Robert Keating's extraordinary article "Live Aid: The Terrible Truth." *Spin*. Web. July. 1986.

http://www.spin.com/featured/live-aid-the-terrible-truth-ethiopia-bob-geldof-feature/

Information about the *We Are the World* effort came from Jess Cagle's article "We Are the World." *Entertainment Weekly*. 24 Jan. 1992. Web. http://www.ew.com/article/1992/01/24/we-are-world

Information about the charitable efforts of *We Are the World* came from this source: Staff. "Record's First Profits Will Go To The Hungry." *The New York Times*. 19 May. 1985. Web. http://www.nytimes.com/1985/05/19/arts/record-s-first-profits-will-go-to-the-hungry.html?sec=&spon=

A wonderful description of each of the concerts came from Graham Jones' article "Live Aid 1985: A Day Of Magic." CNN.com. 6 July. 2005 Web. http://edition.cnn.com/2005/SHOWBIZ/Music/07/01/liveaid.memories/index.html

Hippocratic oath information came from the U.S. National Library of Medicine. *Pubmed.gov*. 27 Sep. 2016. Web. http://www.ncbi.nlm.nih.gov/pubmed

The Advantages of Color Blindness
Emerson Moser's story came from this website reference: "Twenty Famous Color-Blind People: They Rock Despite Having the Color Handicap." *Improveeyesighthq.com* Web. http://www.improveeyesighthq.com/famous-color-blind-people.html

Momentary Lapse of Reason: Fear

The five fear categories came from Dr. Karl Albrecht's enlightening article "The Only 5 Fears We All Share." *Psychology Today*. 22 Mar. 2012. Web. https://www.psychologytoday.com/blog/brainsnacks/201203 /the-only-5-fears-we-all-share. I refer to these fears through-out the book, but provide a thorough explanation in the *Momentary Lapse of Reason: Fear* section.

Chapter 9

A Bird in the Hand...

David Ropeik writes about the *loss aversion* and *risk perception* concepts in his article "Are These Dangerous Times, or Do They Just Feel That Way?" *Psychology Today*. 2 Jan. 2015. Web. https://www.psychologytoday.com/blog/how-risky-is-it-re-ally/201501/are-these-dangerous-times-or-do-they-just-feel-way

The National Geographic reference came from here: "Flash Facts About Lightning." *National Geographic*. Updated 24 Jun. 2005. Web. http://news.nationalgeographic.com/news/2004/06/0623_04 0623_lightningfacts.html

The shark attack statistic came from Thomas Barrabi's article "After Air Algerie AH5017 Incident, a Statistical Look at the Probability and Chances of Dying in a Plane Crash." *International Business Times.* 24 Jul. 2014. Web. http://www.ibtimes.com/after-air-algerie-ah5017-incident-statistical-look-probability-chances-dying-plane-crash-1638206. Arnold Barnett's quote also came from this article.

The death probabilities came from the National Safety Council. "Odds of Dying From..." *Injury Facts, 2014 Edition.* National Safety Council. Web. http://www.nsc.org/NSCDocuments_Corporate/2014-Injury-Facts-Odds-Dying-43.pdf

Counting Cards
"Gambling." Dictionary.com. Unabridged. Random House, Inc. 20 Apr. 2015. Web. http://www.dictionary.com/browse/gambling?s=t

"Chance." Dictionary.com. Unabridged. Random House, Inc. 20 Apr. 2015. Web. http://www.dictionary.com/browse/chance?s=t

American Gaming Association's data and quote came from their website: www.americangaming.org. 20 Apr. 2015. Web.

The gambling dollar estimates came from Jordan Weissmann's article "Is Illegal Sports Betting a $400 Billion Industry?" *Inc.com*. 21 Nov. 2014. Web.
http://www.inc.com/slate/jordan-weissmann-is-illegal-sports-betting-a-400-billion-industry.html

Ben Mezrich's book reference: *Bringing Down the House: The Inside Story of Six M.I.T. Students Who Took Vegas for Millions*. Free Press, 2002. Print.

The Tech article quote referenced was written by Jenny Zhang. "Card Counting Gig Nets Students Millions." *The Tech*. 25 Oct. 2002. Web. http://tech.mit.edu/V122/N50/50bj.50n.html

The card counting techniques and descriptions came from "How to Count Cards." Blackjackapprenticeship.com. 11 Nov. 2016. Web.
https://www.blackjackapprenticeship.com/resources/how-to-count-cards/

Go For It! What We Can Learn From The Coach Who Never Punts

The information about Coach Kevin Kelley and the Pulaski Academy football program came from the following three references:

Staples, Andy. "The Power of Not Punting: Why a College Coach Should Adopt Kevin Kelley's Unconventional Philosophy." *Campus Rush* by *Sports Illustrated*. 09 Sep. 2015. Web.
http://www.campusrush.com/kevin-kelley-pulaski-academy-power-of-not-punting-1338619200.html

Staff. "The High School Football Coach Who Never Punts." *FiveThirtyEight*. 16 Dec. 2015. Web.
http://fivethirtyeight.com/features/the-high-school-football-coach-who-never-punts/

The quotes from coaches came from Keith Jarrett's article "High School Coach Who Never Punts, Always Onside Kicks." *Citizen-Times (Asheville)*. 13 Oct. 2014. Web.
http://www.citizen-times.com/story/sports/2014/10/13/high-school-coach-never-punts-always-onside-kicks/17213961/

Vacc-A-Phobia
Information about the opposition to the smallpox vaccination and on the virus itself came from Derrick Baxby's article "End of Smallpox." *History Today*. vol. 49 Issue 3. March 1999 Mar 1999. Web.
http://www.historytoday.com/derrick-baxby/end-smallpox

Information about the history of vaccines came from The College of Physicians of Philadelphia: "History of Smallpox." www.historyofvaccines.org 3 May 2015. Web.
http://www.historyofvaccines.org/content/articles/history-smallpox

The NPR quote about polio came from Jason Beaubien's article "Wiping Out Polio: How The U.S. Snuffed Out a Killer." *NPR.com*. 15 Oct. 2012. Web.
http://www.npr.org/sections/health-shots/2012/10/16/162670836/wiping-out-polio-how-the-u-s-snuffed-out-a-killer

Information about Salk and later Sabin's vaccines for polio came from this source: Staff. "March 26, 1953: Salk Announces Polio Vaccine." *History.com*. 2010. 4 May 2015. Web.
http://www.history.com/this-day-in-history/salk-announces-polio-vaccine

The information on measles came from the CDC: "Measles—Q&A About Disease & Vaccine." *CDC.gov*. 6 May 2015. Web.
http://www.cdc.gov/vaccines/vpd-vac/measles/faqs-dis-vac-risks.htm

The information about mumps came from webmd.com: "Mumps." www.webmd.com. 6 May 2015. Web.
http://www.webmd.com/children/tc/mumps-topic-overview

The Mayo Clinic quote about rubella came from this resource: Staff. "Rubella Complications." www.mayoclinic.org. 6 May 2015. Web.
http://www.mayoclinic.org/diseases-condi-tions/rubella/basics/complications/con-20020067

The data about the illnesses and deaths that resulted from rubella came from this source: www.historyofvaccines.org 6 May 2015. Web.
http://www.historyofvaccines.org/content/articles/rubella

MMR vaccination information came from "Measles, Mumps, and Rubella (MMR) Vaccine." Children's Vaccines. www.webmd.com. 6 May 2015. Web.
http://www.webmd.com/children/vaccines/measles-mumps-and-rubella-mmr-vaccine

The information about Mr. Wakefield falsifying records and data came from Vanessa Wamsley's article "The Psychology of Anti-Vaxers: How Story Trumps Science." *The Atlantic*. 19 Oct. 2014. Web.
http://www.theatlantic.com/health/archive/2014/10/how-anti-vaccine-fear-takes-hold/381355/. This article was also the source of Dr. Hendrix's quote.

The quote about the association between MMR and autism came from this source: "MMR Vaccine & Autism." www.aap.org. Immunization. 5 May 2015. Web.
https://www2.aap.org/immunization/families/mmr.html

The diagnosis data and quote came from this source: Autism. "Autism Fact Sheet." *National Institute of Neurological Disorders and Stroke.* Sep. 2009. www.ninds.nih.gov. 6 May 2015. Web. http://www.ninds.nih.gov/disorders/autism/detail_autism.htm

The diagnosis doubling information came from the CDC. "Autism Spectrum Disorder (ASD)." Data & Statistics. Centers for Disease Control and Prevention. *www.CDC.gov.* 6 May 2015. Web. http://www.cdc.gov/ncbddd/autism/data.html

The concept of what causes the fear of vaccination came in part from David Ropeik's "On the Persistence and Underlying Causes of Vax-O-Noia." *Psychology Today.* 2/13 Feb. 2015. Web. https://www.psychologytoday.com/blog/how-risky-is-it-really/201502/the-persistence-and-underlying-causes-vax-o-noia

On The Flip Side Of Risk Aversion
Information about the *endowment effect* came from Gizem Saka's article "Loss Aversion: Why Do We Hang onto Things for No Reason?" *Psychology Today.* 31 Aug. 2011. Web. https://www.psychologytoday.com/blog/the-decision-lab/201108/loss-aversion-why-do-we-hang-things-no-reason

Dr. Cialdini's quote came from his book *Influence, Science and Practice.* 5th ed. Boston: Pearson Education Inc., 2009. Print. 214.

Risk aversion of perfectionists came from Preston Ni's article "8 Negative Attitudes of Chronically Unhappy People." *Psychology Today.* 22 Feb. 2015. Web.
https://www.psychologytoday.com/blog/communication-success/201502/8-negative-attitudes-chronically-unhappy-people

INDEX

American Savings Education Council, 30

Activision, 95

Actor-observer bias, 156

Adjacency, 165

Aerospatiale, 151

Air France, 151-153

Albrecht, Karl, 181, 191

Alien (the movie), 91

American Academy of Pediatrics, 211

Analysis paralysis, 12, 110

Analytical system, 12, 194, 221

Apple, Inc., 104

Association, The Principle of, 46, 73, 76, 79, 83, 85, 90-91, 94, 103-104, 107, 113, 211

Asteroids, 92

Astor, Mrs. William Backhouse, 36

Astraphobia, 190-191

Atari, 90, 92-96

Authority, 38-39, 46, 57, 59-60

Autism Spectrum Disorder (ASD), 209-211, 213

Autopilot system (Autopilot), 5, 12-13, 20, 47, 53-54, 75-76, 78, 110, 115, 126-127, 134, 157-158, 161, 182, 221-222

Aviophobia, 190-191

Banco Zarossi, 145

Band Aid (organization), 167-168

BAND-AID (bandages), 127

Bar mixer, 111

Battlestar Galactica, 91

Because (as a justifier), 18-22, 42-44

Behavioral economics, 11

Belief perseverance, 156

Benjamin Franklin, An American Life, 63

Berman, Jillian, 30

Biases, 2, 11, 13, 20, 31, 53, 65, 68, 74-76, 78, 85, 99-100, 106, 127, 130-131, 156, 161-162, 166, 177, 181

Blind obedience, 38

Body language, 4, 68-72

Bounded rationality, 11

Bowie, David, 168

British Aircraft Corporation, 151

British Airways, 151-152

British Medical Journal, 210

Buck Rogers in the 25th Century, 91

Burger King uniform study, 60-61

Buzzword Bingo, 117-121, 129

Calculated risk, 96, 198, 218-219

Canadian Warehousing Company, 146

Card counting, 194-195, 197-198

Case study (approach), 131

Causation, 77-79, 96, 103

Centers for Disease Control and Prevention (CDC), 207, 210

Chemical Bank, 36

Chinese Exclusion Act, 86

Choice-supportive bias, 177

Cialdini, Robert, 216

Citizen-Times (Asheville), 202

Close Encounters of the Third Kind, 91

CNN, 122

Coburn, Tom, 122

Coca-Cola (The Coca-Cola Company), 83, 128

Cochran, Johnny, 128-129

Cognitive psychology, 11

ColecoVision, 95

Colorblindness, 173-175, 178

Compare/contrast, 44-46, 73-74

Complex (psychological), 100

Concorde, 150-153

Confirmatory bias, 20, 161

The Conference Board, 29

Conjunction fallacy, 79

Conscientious objector, 204

Consistency, 21, 41, 43, 116, 127-129, 161-162, 177

Conspicuous consumption, 36

Consumer Confidence Index, 29

Contrast principle, 74

Controlled responding, 54

Copy Machine Study, 18

Correlation, 77-80, 89, 94, 96-97, 101, 103

Crotty, James Marshall, 33

Dale, Stacy, 101

Dance Fever, 174

Deer, Brian, 210

The Definitive Book of Body Language, 70

Democrat, 54, 123

Double down, 135, 149, 153-154, 156

Dr. Fox Effect, 57, 59-60, 120

E.F. Hutton, 81

E.T. the Extra-Terrestrial, 91-96

E*Trade, 26

Ego death, 139, 182, 192

Employee Benefit Research Institute, 30

Endowment effect, 215

Etcoff, Nancy, 60, 98-99, 116

Ethiopia, 166, 168-172

Exception fallacy, 52

Executive Order 9066, 87

Expectations, 43, 74, 79, 126, 130

Expert/expertise, 38, 46, 59-60, 64, 70, 75, 120

Extinction, 181, 191-192

Eye contact, 71-72

Fallacies, 11, 13, 52-53, 75, 79, 101, 103, 107, 140

False cause, 77-78, 85, 94, 103

Familiarity, 111, 115-116, 122, 124, 126-127, 130, 176

Fear, 47, 105, 139, 179-183, 190-192, 198, 204, 210-214, 217, 219, 222

Federal Reserve Bank of St. Louis, 30

Fidelity Investments, 30

Five fear categories, 191

Forbes, 32-33, 80, 101

Ford, 16

Foreign Miner Tax, 86

Franklin, Benjamin, 63

FRED Economic Data, 30

Frogger, 92

Frogmen, 61-63

Functional fixedness bias, 162, 166

Galeophobia, 190-191

Gallup poll, 123

Game theory, 57-59

Gebicki, Michael, 151

Gekko, Gordon, 186, 188

Geldof, Bob, 166-168, 170-172

Giberti, Ettore, 148

Gorbachev, Mikhail, 172

Greene, Robert, 73

Guccione, Bob, 170

Halo effect, 66, 177

Heitler, Susan, 99

Hendrix, Kristin, 212

Heuristics, 12, 20, 40, 59, 63, 161

Hierarchy of dominance, 98

Hindsight bias, 130-131

Homer, 39

Honda, 16

HubSpot, 26

Huffington Post, 30

Ideal self, 18, 21, 44

Ideology, 44, 124-125

Illusion-of-truth effect, 129

Illusory correlation, 82

In-group bias, 85

Indiana University School of Medicine, 212

Inflexibility, 161-162, 172-173, 175-176, 178

Inoculation, 204-206, 213

Inquiry (publication), 205

Intellivision, 95

International Reply Coupons, 147-148

IQ, 96-97

Isaacson, Walter, 63

Iverson, Allen, 33

J. Walter Thompson, 81-83, 104

Jackson, Michael, 167

Jaffe, Chuck, 31

Jannot, Jeannine, 3

Jarrett, Keith, 202

Jenner, Edward, 205

Jones, Elizabeth Schermer-horn, 36

Jones, Quincy, 167

The Jonses of New York, 36

Journal of Medical Education, 58

Jung, Carl, 13-14

Just-world phenomenon, 107

Justifications/justifying, 15, 17, 19-22, 24-25, 28-29, 31-32, 37-45, 78, 106-108, 115, 123, 155-156, 187-189

Kahneman, Daniel, 128

Kassar, Ray, 93

Kelley, Kevin, 199-204, 117

Key differentiating factor, 45

King Solomon, 72

Kit Kat, 128

Klein, Gary, 27-28

Knuckleheads, 9

Krueger, Alan, 101

Lag effect, 129

The Lancet, 209-210

Langer, Ellen, 18, 20

Levine, Beth, 125

Levy, Gary, 60

Live Aid, 166-168, 170-172

Los Angeles Times, 88

Loss aversion, 189, 193

Loss of Autonomy, 182, 192

Lowe, Jock, 151

M&Ms, 128

Magnavox, 95

Marcinko, Richard, 62-63

Mariam, Mengistu Haile, 169-172

Market Watch, 31

Mattel, 95

Maxwell House, 128

Mayo Clinic, 208

Mazda, 16

McLuhan, Marshall, 68

Measles, 207-208, 210, 212-213

Members Only, 34-35, 37, 44, 155

Meow Mix, 128

Mercedes-Benz, 22, 24-26, 41, 90

Mere-exposure effect, 116, 120

Mirroring, 25, 72

MIT, 26-27, 190, 194-196, 198, 218

Momentary Lapses of Reason, 5, 47, 75, 109, 132, 157, 159, 179, 191, 221

Montagu, Lady Mary Wortley, 204

Moser, Emerson, 173

Ms. Pac-Man, 92, 95-96

Mumps, 207-208, 210, 212-213

Mutilation, 182, 192

Napoleon complex, 100

National Bureau of Economic Research, 29

National Institute of Neurological Disorders and Stroke, 209

NBA, 33, 193

NFL, 33-34

Nissan, 16

Normative decision theory, 1

Odysseus, 39-40

The Odyssey, 39

Odyssey 2 (game console), 95

On The Flip Side, 1, 4, 10, 40-41, 66, 103, 127, 153, 175, 214, 222

Optimism bias, 31

Oscar Mayer, 127

Ostrich effect, 31

Parkinson's disease, 125-126

Patriarchs Ball, 36

Pavlov's dogs, 90

Payscale.com, 101

Pease, Allan and Barbara, 70

Perceptual contrast principle, 59

Perfectionists, 217

Personal savings rate, 30, 32

Phillips, Todd, 124

Pitfall!, 90, 92

Placebo (effect), 79, 105, 126

Polio (aka Infant Paralysis), 205-206, 212

Pong, 92

Ponzi scheme, 143

Ponzi, Charles (Carlo), 143-150

Position power, 38, 46

Power of extra effort, 155

Pride of authorship, 176

Princeton University, 88-89, 200

Proof of concept, 131

Proof of quality, 25

Provenzano, Frank, 3

Psychological reactance, 216

Pulaski Academy, 199-203

Raiders of the Lost Ark, 92

Reimagine, 118

Replacement terms, 117

Representative heuristic, 59, 63

Republican, 54, 123

Retail therapy, 16, 158, 215

Richie, Lionel, 167

Risk (aversion), 4, 96, 139, 175-176, 185, 188-194, 196, 198, 200, 203-204, 208, 210-211, 213-215, 219

Roese, Neal, 131

The Rogue Warrior, 62

Roosevelt, Franklin D., 87, 181

Rosy retrospection, 176

Rubella, 207-208, 210, 210, 212-213

Sabin, Albert, 206

Salk, Jonas, 206

Samson, Alain, 120

Sassa, Scott, 52-54

Seinfeld, 119

Selassie, Haile, 169

Self-concept, 107-108

Self-esteem, 73-74, 85, 99

Self-fulfilling prophecy, 105

Self-identity, 17, 21, 41, 43-44, 156

Self-respect, 67

Self-serving attribution bias, 106

Sensation transference, 116

Separation, 139, 182, 192

Seredy, Kate, 179

Shyong, Frank, 88-89

Simpson, O.J., 128-129

Siren's Call, 39-40

Sloan School of Management, 26-27

Smallpox, 204-206, 212

Smile, 70-71

Snowbirds, 77

Social comparison, 25

Social proof, 60, 120, 130, 176

Soelberg, Peer, 27-28

Sonic boom, 152

Sources of Power, 27

Space 1999, 91

Space Invaders, 92

Spacing effect, 129

Spielberg, Steven, 91-93

Spin Magazine, 170

Sports Illustrated, 33

Spurious correlation, 79

Star Trek, 91

Star Wars, 91

Status symbol, 37, 61

Steinhauser, Paul, 122

Stereotype/stereotyping, 16, 33, 49, 52-54, 59, 62-63, 65-66, 76, 85-88, 98, 209, 222

Success stories, 175-176

Sunk cost (fallacy), 138, 140, 142, 154-156

Survival of the Prettiest, 60

Tall Man Syndrome, 99

The 48 Laws of Power, 73

The Four Hundred, 36-37

The Great Recession, 29-30

The Securities Exchange Company, 148, 150

The Tipping Point, 118

Thin-slicing, 63

Time pressure, 47, 54, 132-134, 197, 222

Townsend, John Marshall, 60

Toyota, 16-17, 22

Turner Advertising, 49

Turner Broadcasting System, 49

Turner, Ted, 51

Twain, Mark, 97

U.S. Bureau of Labor Statistics, 96

U.S. Navy SEALs, 61

Underhill, Paco, 39, 165

Underwater Demolition Teams (UDTs), 61

United States House of Representatives, 121

United States Navy, 61-62, 173

United States Senate, 121

United Support of Artists for Africa, 167

University of Cincinnati, 125

University of Pittsburgh, 206

Ure, Midge, 167

Vaccination (source), 205-213

Valence effect, 31

Victim mentality, 107-108

Victoria's Secret, 82-84

Vohs, Kathleen, 131

Wakefield, Andrew, 209-210

Wall Street (movie), 186

Warshaw, Howard Scott, 91-94, 96, 106

Wheaties, 128

Why We Buy (book), 39, 165

Wichita Falls Motor Company, 146

World Health Organization, 205

Yars' Revenge, 92

Yoon, Robert, 122

Zarossi, Luigi, 145

Zipcar, 26

Zuckoff, Mitchell, 145

PERSUADED

Made in the USA
San Bernardino, CA
03 November 2017